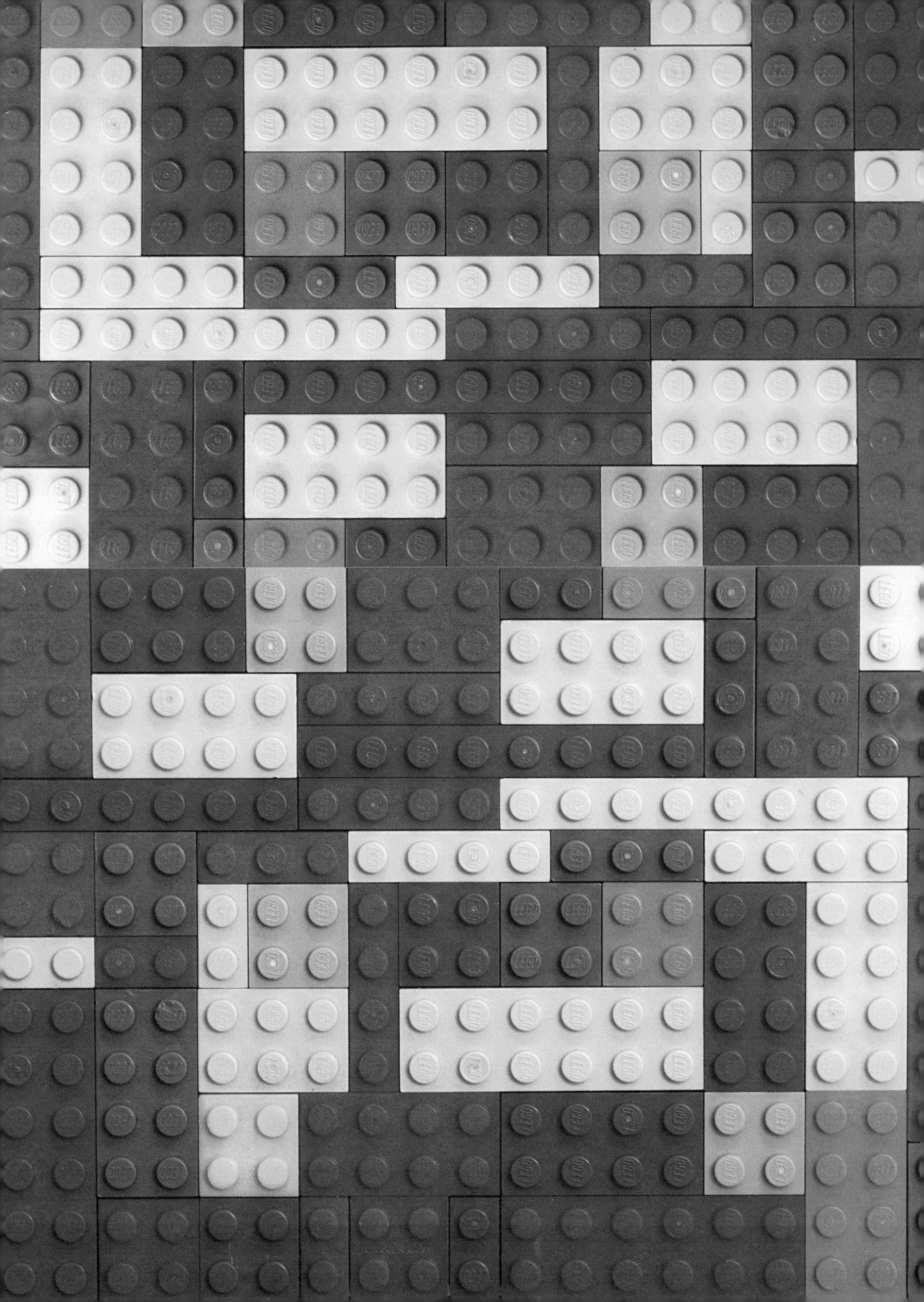

THE TOY THAT CHANGED OUR LIVES

Just in time for the 20th anniversary of the partnership between the LEGO universe and the Star Wars galaxy, the LEGO Group introduced the Star Wars BOOST Droid Commander. The set gives builders the opportunity to build working droids.

A WORLD IN A BOX

Opening the box of a new LEGO set is a cultural touchstone in countries all over the world. In that moment, an adventure lies before every child, every parent, as well as every grown-up finding that old inspirations can become new again. A challenge, a puzzle, a chance to bond with friends and family, a forum for all the imagination that might otherwise just fly out of our heads and into the ether: the LEGO System of Play is all of these and more. In this collection, created in concert with the LEGO Corporation, we'll explore the greatest playsets and builds in history, and reveal why, in many respects, the best is still yet to come.

The LEGO minifigure, which was released in 1978, was the brainchild of Jens Nygaard Knudsen, who had been working with the LEGO Group for nearly 10 years when he had his game-changing idea. Knudsen passed away in February 2020.

CONTENTS

In 1962, at Selfridges department store in London, 6-year-old Philippa Smith takes part in an interactive LEGO brick display. LEGO bricks had been available in the U.K. two years earlier.

KENT GAVIN/KEYSTONE/HULTON ARCHIVE/GETTY IMAGES

The Story of LEGO

For more than a century, the company started by Ole Kirk Kristiansen has been obsessed with quality.

1916

Ole Kirk Kristiansen (below) purchases the Billund Maskinsnedkeri (joinery factory). According to the LEGO Group, the factory "makes doors, windows, kitchen cabinets, cupboards, coffins, chests of drawers, tools for digging peat and bodywork for carts."

1924

While Ole Kirk and his wife, Kristine, enjoy a nap, their sons accidentally set fire to the factory. No one is injured but both the factory and the Kirk home are destroyed.

1949

The first "automatic binding bricks," the precursor to the LEGO brick, are released by the LEGO Group.

1940

1950

1934

Just two years after the Depression forces Ole Kirk to fire his last journeyman, the wooden toys he began producing with the help of his sons are christened after the Danish phrase "LEg GOdt," meaning "play well,." They are deemed worthy of an exhibition space by the National Association for Danish Enterprise.

1942

Ole Kirk continues making toys after the outbreak of World War II, but three years before the conflict's end, his factory suffers another fire. This time, the adjoining home is saved.

Patent drawings for LEGO bricks show the interlocking mechanism.

1950

1951
LEGO Mursten (LEGO Bricks) is added to "automatic binding bricks" on packaging to increase exposure of the brand name.

1953
Beginning with a partnership with plastic manufacturers, the LEGO Group begins spreading across the Nordic countries.

1955
The first product marketed as part of the LEGO System in Play is launched, encouraging children to build houses out of LEGO bricks.

1956 –1958
The LEGO Group expands its operations throughout Europe.

1958
After Ole Kirk's death, Godtfred Kirk Christiansen helms the LEGO Group.

1960

1960
After yet another fire, the LEGO Group ceases production of wooden toys altogether.

1961
After the LEGO Group makes a deal with the American company Shwayder, manufacturers of Samsonite luggage, LEGO bricks make their American debut.

1962
The LEGO Wheel is introduced at the Nuremberg Toy Fair.

1963
The first building instructions for LEGO sets are created.

1967
Dagny Holm is asked to create a LEGO train for Tivoli Gardens in Copenhagen, one of the world's oldest theme parks. The following year, after six years of development, LEGOLAND family park opens in Billund, largely inspired by and featuring Holm's designs.

1969
DUPLO bricks are first introduced by the LEGO Group. They will become their own branded system in 1978.

1974
The first molding factory outside of Denmark, in Baar, Switzerland, opens.

1978
LEGO Space debuts.

1979
Kjeld Kirk Kristiansen becomes president of the company.

1982
The Expert Builder series matures and becomes Technic; the LEGO Group celebrates its 50th anniversary.

1970 · 1980 · 1985

1978
The LEGO Minifigure makes its debut; LEGO Castle series is launched.

1987
Forestmen and Crusaders, sub-lines of LEGO Castle, are introduced. Blacktron I and Futuron, sub-lines of LEGO Space, are introduced.

1988
The first LEGO World Cup building contest is held in Billund.

1989
The LEGO Pirates theme is introduced.

1995
Godtfred Kirk Christiansen dies.

1996
LEGOLAND Windsor opens in the U.K.; *lego.com* is launched. The following year, its first computer game is released.

1998
The LEGO Group introduces the earliest iteration of MINDSTORMS.

1999
LEGOLAND California opens in Carlsbad; LEGO Star Wars makes its debut in stores.

2001
LEGO Harry Potter is introduced.

1985 · 1990 · 2000

2000
The British Association of Toy Retailers names the LEGO brick "Toy of the Century."

2002
LEGOLAND Deutschland opens.

2006
LEGO Batman and Spongebob Squarepants debut. The previous year saw the addition of Vikings.

2008
LEGO Ideas makes its trial run in Japan. Soon it will be incorporating fan ideas into purchasable sets.

2010

2011
Along with a range of new branded tie-ins including Pirates of the Caribbean, LEGO NINJAGO is introduced.

2012
LEGO The Lord of the Rings and The Hobbit are introduced.

2014
THE LEGO MOVIE premieres.

2017
The *LEGO Batman* and *NINJAGO* movies premiere. The combined gross of the three LEGO film properties will eventually reach $904,192,631.

2020

An early LEGO wooden toy locomotive on display at the company's headquarters in Billund, Denmark.

How the Brick is Made

Henrik Østergaard Nielsen speaks to *Newsweek* from the LEGO molding factory in Billund, Denmark, and reveals the process behind making the world's most famous (and prolific) brick.

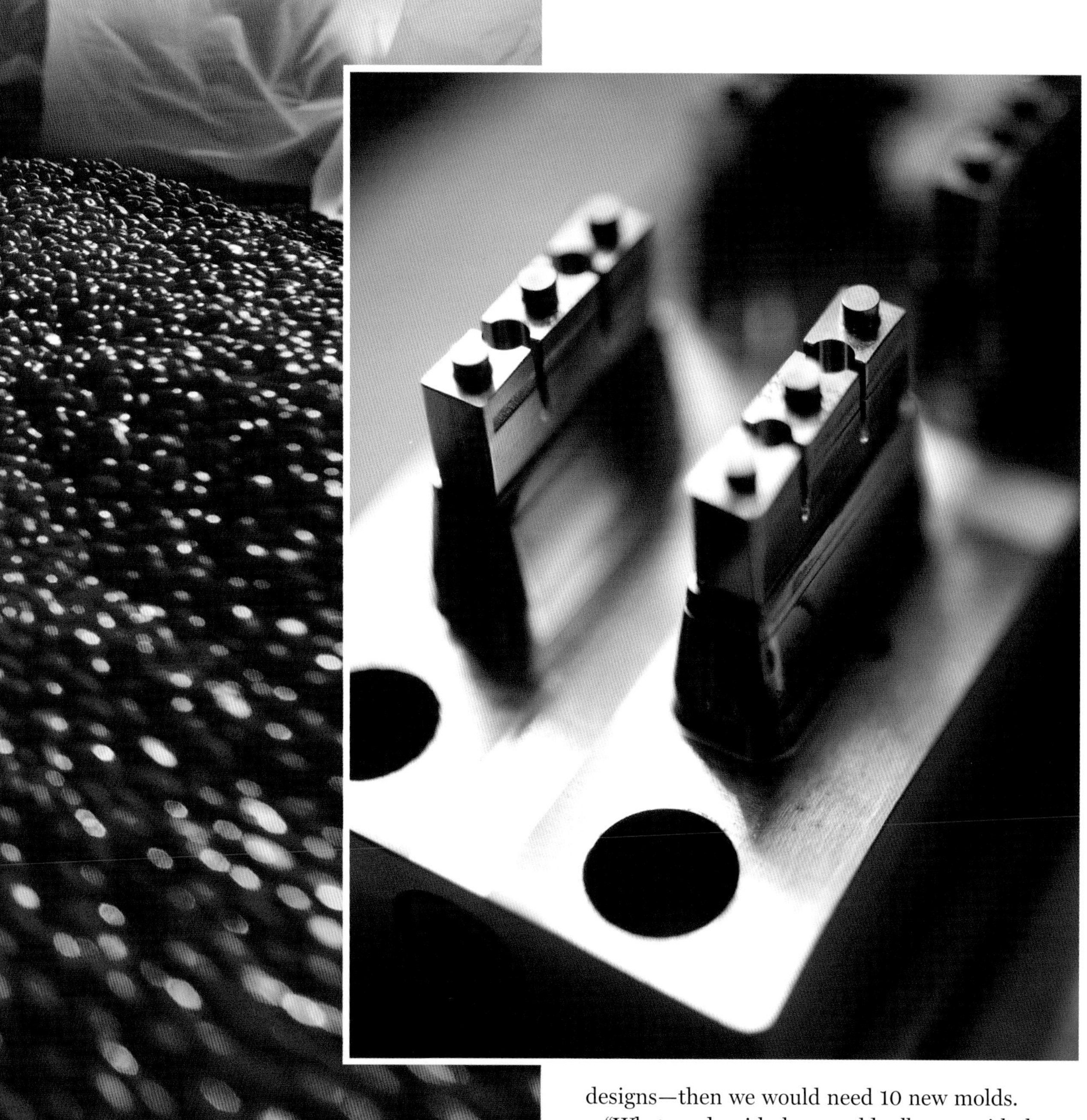

“I’M HERE in The LEGO Group’s molding factory in Billund, where we actually mold the LEGO bricks. An idea [for a set and its pieces] would normally go to our engineering department, who would then develop tools for us. They actually design and manufacture a mold [for each necessary piece] that is accurate to within the width of a single hair. Once that tool has been approved, after a lot of testing and measurement, we receive a tool (pictured above right) for each LEGO element. So if in a new set you have 10 new LEGO bricks—10 new designs—then we would need 10 new molds.

“What we do with those molds all starts with the resin, the raw pellets of plastic (pictured above left). The process begins with melting the plastic at around 235 degrees Celsius (455 degrees Fahrenheit), when it becomes like toothpaste in density. We take that into the mold and cool it down to about 60 degrees Celsius (140 degrees Fahrenheit), and then you actually have the finished LEGO brick.

“Molding is all about efficiency. We are not looking into ‘Are we producing fire stations or police stations?’ We are simply producing billions of bricks, then they are shipped to the next process in the supply chain. Of course, there have been improvements to the process—how could we get more output, for example—but the process itself has really not changed since the beginning.”

LIANG SEN/XINHUA/ALAMY

At the 2017 BrickCan, Canada's largest LEGO convention, people take a closer look at a LEGO Batcave consisting of more than 20,000 pieces. The build weighs more than 100 pounds.

LEGO Brick Learning

The LEGO Foundation is dedicated to putting LEGO bricks to a noble use in classrooms around the world.

IN BILLUND, DENMARK, and Baar, Switzerland, The LEGO Foundation may well be ensuring the future of the LEGO Group through their tireless work toward incorporating LEGO bricks into as many educational models as possible. Sarah Bouchie, head of Learning Through Play in Early Childhood at The LEGO Foundation, is spearheading the idea that playtime isn't something to allow children as a reward for learning—it is the most important aspect of learning. "I think what's important is that we're helping to give strategies to our partners about how they facilitate play," Bouchie explains. "There's free play that allows children to be imaginative and creative on their own. Then there's directed play—think about things like games and sports where there are defined rules. And then there's this sweet spot in between, which we call guided play." This engaging form of play involves helping children along as they experiment, talking through causes and effects while still maintaining the imagination-based and relatively carefree feeling of unbridled playtime.

Rob Lowe, senior director of Kids Engagement at the LEGO Group, reinforces this focus the LEGO System in Play puts on cooperation and communication. "That experience of building together—me searching for the bricks and my daughter building and then swapping around—I can spend hours doing that. We talk while doing it, and then she does some roleplaying with the set she's built." This leads to a sense of working together to accomplish a goal that Lowe, a LEGO fan whose

On average, during the holiday shopping season, 28 LEGO sets are sold every second, according to *National Geographic Kids*.

At a Block Kids building event hosted by the National Association of Women in Construction at Gage Elementary School in Rochester, Minnesota, student Tara Covault builds a structure with LEGO bricks that will be judged by local construction industry members. Insets: Rob Lowe and Sarah Bouchie.

habit has followed him from DUPLO bricks to a career at the company, and whose most prized possession is a still-in-the-box 1980s LEGO Space set, never tires of. But more importantly, it leads to an important side effect of guided play that makes the LEGO brick a particularly good medium. Once children discover that LEGO bricks allow them to both create their own worlds and combine their favorite pre-existing fictional ones, the imaginative effects can be remarkable. "More recently, she started taking fragments of sets—a cockpit from a spaceship or a bit from a car—and then building a house out of it," Lowe continues. "And she's showing some of the skill techniques that the LEGO designers have in building her own kind of

RIGHT: ANDREW LINK/THE ROCHESTER

"Not only is it cognitive skills [we're honing], but if you ask the children to wait, for example, until a tower they've created falls, they're so excited."

—SARAH BOUCHIE, HEAD OF LEARNING THROUGH PLAY IN EARLY CHILDHOOD AT THE LEGO FOUNDATION

Frankenstein's monster creations."

This leap forward in imaginative capability, according to Bouchie, can in turn lead to forums for the introduction of other important life skills through play. "Not only is it cognitive skills [we're honing], but if you ask the children to wait, for example, until a tower they've created falls, they're

Students in Naperville, Illinois, compete in a LEGO League tournament sponsored by FIRST, which stands for, For Inspiration and Recognition of Science and Technology. Inset: The LEGO characteristics of play include: iterative, which shows the value of trying out new possibilities; meaningful, which grounds play in the real world; socially interactive; joyful; and actively engaged.

RIGHT: DAVID SHAROS/CHICAGO TRIBUNE/TNS/NEWSCOM

so excited," she says. But that excitement is also an opportunity for a teaching moment. "They're practicing that restraint before they tip something over, which is actually developing the emotional regulation we want to see in young children." The children learn that waiting for the tower to fall on its own is ultimately more satisfying than knocking it over, which can help them realize that sometimes instant gratification isn't what they really want.

While more progressive schools in the West are

opening themselves up to the importance of play in the development of children, Bouchie and The LEGO Foundation's goal is to be able to spread the idea across the world, though they admit that in more traditional pedagogic systems, the idea of play as work has some traction to gain. "This is a different way of working than a lot of classrooms are set up for, where it's more didactic and teacher-directed than child-led," she says. "But the benefits that the children receive are really well-documented." When parents provide early stimulation through guided play, she explains, it reinforces communication between adults and children, provides internal feedback for the child about exactly in which situations to rely on adults and in which they can be more independent. "It promotes bonding that's really important to self-confidence," says Bouchie.

But perhaps the most important thing that guided play teaches children is the feeling of accomplishment they get after imagining something and then creating it in three dimensions. The LEGO Group calls this magic feeling the "pride of creation," and according to Bouchie, this is the magic element that makes guided play "the best way to learn."

During the exhibition *Building Paris from Brick to Brick* at the Paris City Hall in December 2016, children look at a model of the Notre Dame de Paris cathedral.

Architect and LEGO designer Rok Kobe with the New York Skyline set, a 2016 release featuring the Statue of Liberty, Empire State Building, Chrysler Building, Flatiron Building and One World Trade Center.

Real World LEGO Builds

Rok Kobe and his team at the LEGO Group are responsible for one of the company's most ambitious projects, combining the LEGO building system with some of the world's finest architectural marvels.

The Shanghai Skyline LEGO set.

LEGO ARCHITECTURE is, in many ways, an inevitable part of the evolution of the LEGO System in Play. Though the product line doesn't really meet the definition of a "plaything" with its eye toward permanence and attention to historical detail, according to the LEGO Group's Rok Kobe the joy of LEGO Architecture is still in the build. "It's certainly geared toward [being] a display model, but that doesn't mean its beauty is only skin deep," Kobe says. "It doesn't just look good as a model. Where we strive to add value to the model is during the building experience itself."

"Where I strive to design my product, the LEGO Architecture line, is that you try to respect the architect and the ideas behind the building so it's not a simple scale down of a model. It's not just a one-to-one replica that you have in, let's say, a diecast model. You have to abstract a bit more, which gives you the opportunity to represent certain characteristics more acutely."

—ROK KOBE

The latest LEGO brick iteration of the Statue of Liberty includes a more art-deco inspired take on her flowing robes.

INSETS: SHUTTERSTOCK

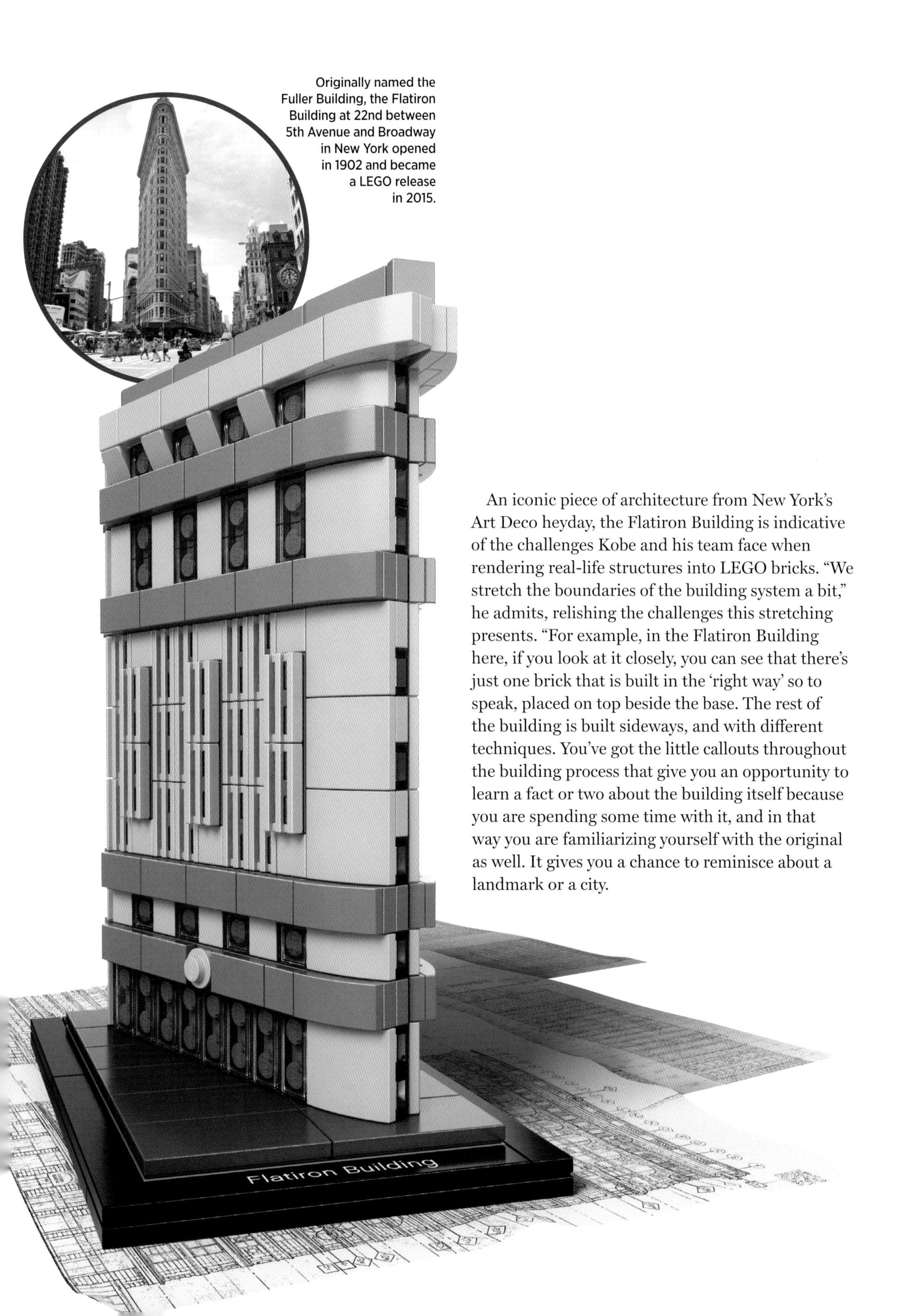

Originally named the Fuller Building, the Flatiron Building at 22nd between 5th Avenue and Broadway in New York opened in 1902 and became a LEGO release in 2015.

An iconic piece of architecture from New York's Art Deco heyday, the Flatiron Building is indicative of the challenges Kobe and his team face when rendering real-life structures into LEGO bricks. "We stretch the boundaries of the building system a bit," he admits, relishing the challenges this stretching presents. "For example, in the Flatiron Building here, if you look at it closely, you can see that there's just one brick that is built in the 'right way' so to speak, placed on top beside the base. The rest of the building is built sideways, and with different techniques. You've got the little callouts throughout the building process that give you an opportunity to learn a fact or two about the building itself because you are spending some time with it, and in that way you are familiarizing yourself with the original as well. It gives you a chance to reminisce about a landmark or a city.

Tokyo's Imperial Hotel (above) was designed by Frank Lloyd Wright to bridge the gap between Eastern and Western concepts of architecture.

"What I try to accent is the original idea of the architect themselves. [Take] the Frank Lloyd Wright Imperial Hotel in Tokyo. Just like with the original, in which he wants to emphasize the Japanese aesthetic qualities of the building, we took that a step further in the LEGO model by [accentuating things like] the perforated roofs." And just like Frank Lloyd Wright, whose designs in earthquake-prone Tokyo required the innovative and experimental to withstand possible tremors, Kobe and his team were faced with smaller-scale versions of real architectural problems, walking a tightrope between architectural design and toy design. "Frank Lloyd Wright designed for an earthquake. In our company, we have something called Model Computal Center because our set has to fulfill certain criteria, just like a real building. For example, when I'm building towers in the skylines, like Shanghai for example, our quality control functions just as a building supervisor would in real life. I have to be careful in every step of the building construction that a tower [with spires as pictured on page 29] doesn't pose a stabbing risk to a child who might fall upon it. It has to be strong enough to endure handling, so that the towers don't topple while you're moving about, but at the same time fragile enough to not pose any risk to any unlucky child who might have an accident."

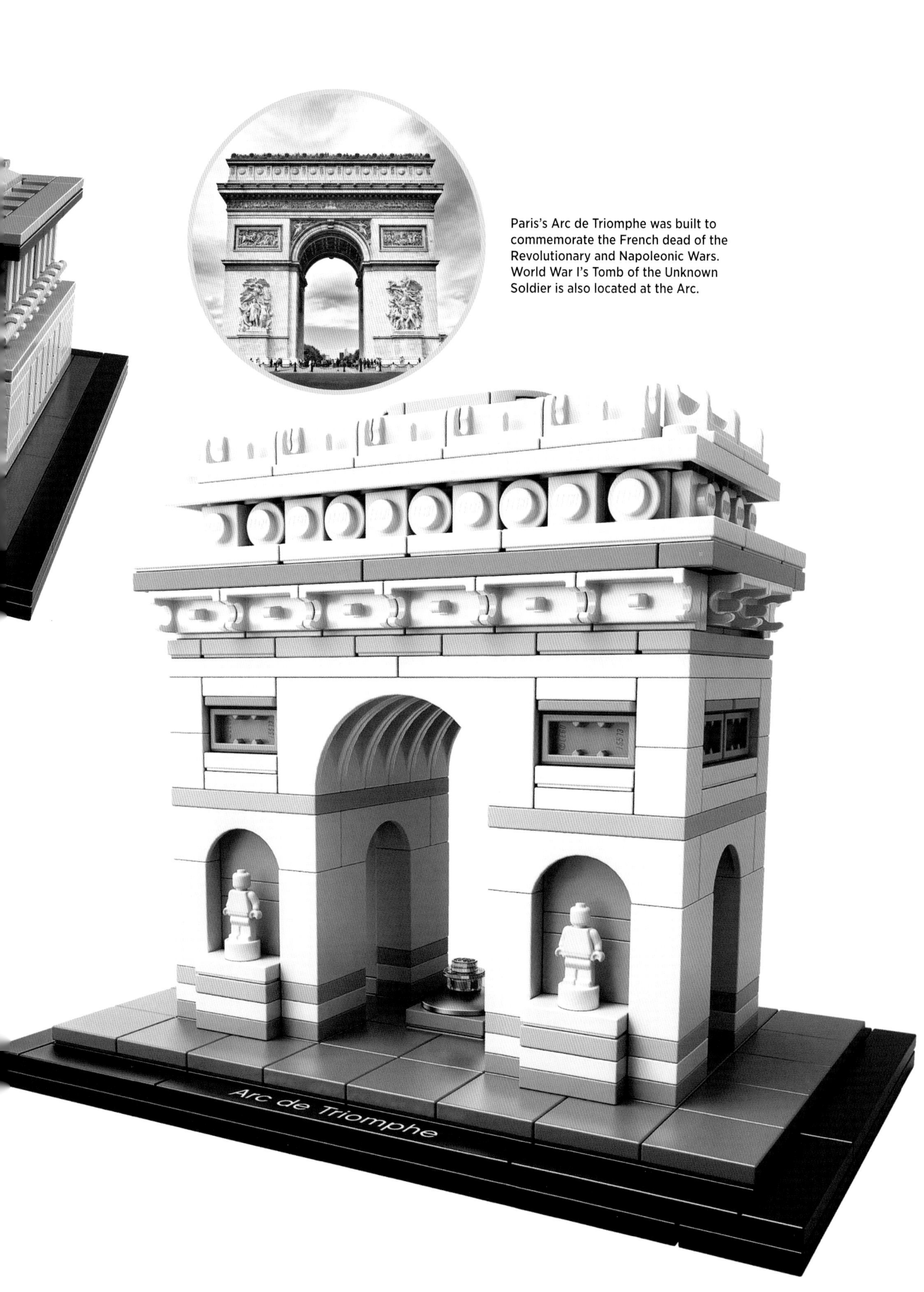

Paris's Arc de Triomphe was built to commemorate the French dead of the Revolutionary and Napoleonic Wars. World War I's Tomb of the Unknown Soldier is also located at the Arc.

Paris's famous Louvre museum, home of masterworks like the Mona Lisa, is the only LEGO Architecture set based on the work of I.M. Pei.

"It's certainly geared toward [being] a display model, but that doesn't mean its beauty is only skin deep. It doesn't just look good as a model. Where we strive to add value to the model is during the building experience itself."

—ROK KOBE

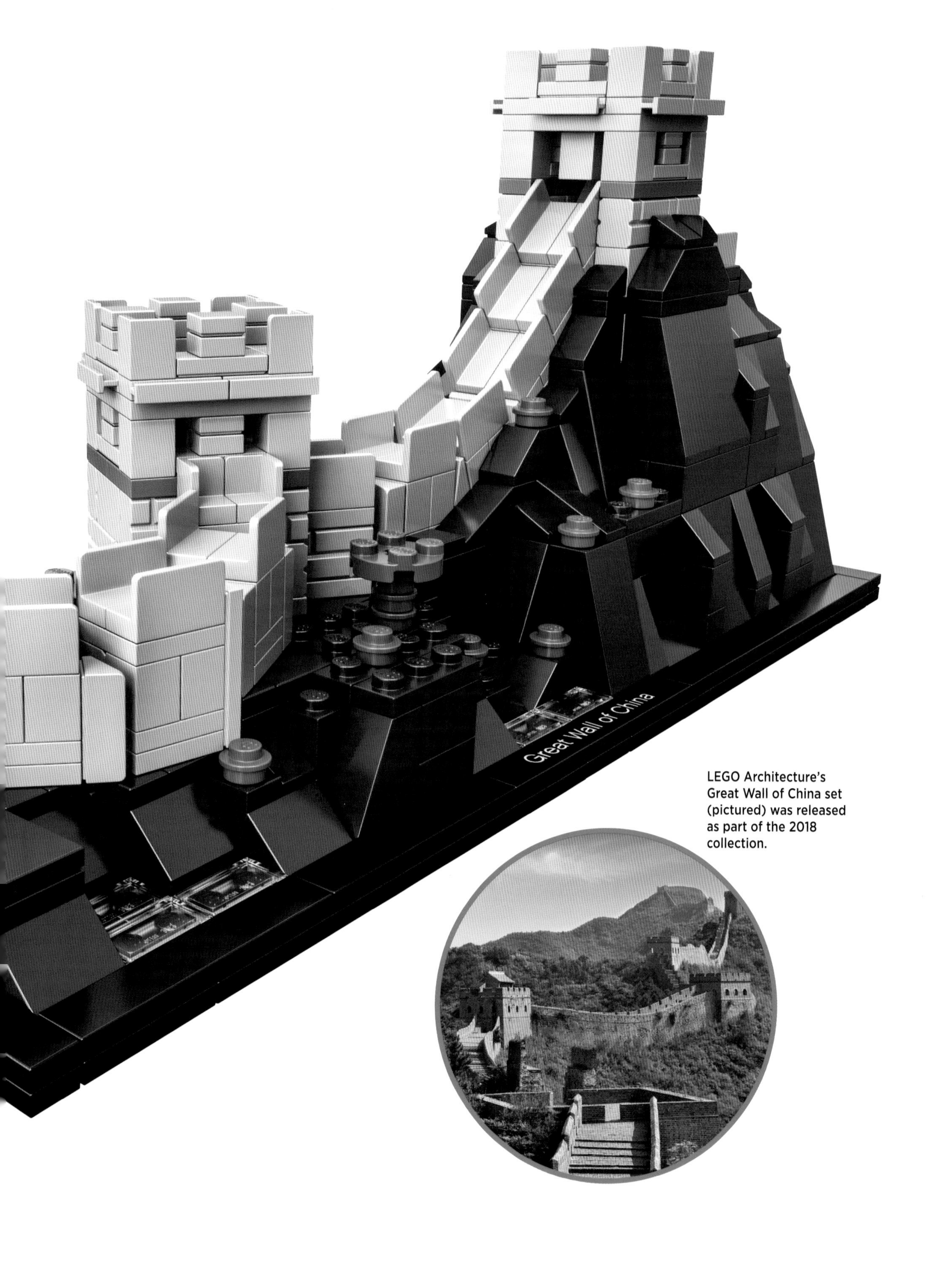

LEGO Architecture's Great Wall of China set (pictured) was released as part of the 2018 collection.

At the National Building Museum in Washington, D.C., patrons admire the LEGO Architecture exhibition in 2010. For insight on LEGO Architecture from its chief designer, turn to page 28.

BUILDING A NEW BRICK

The LEGO Group is going all-in on sustainably producing its products by 2030.

LEGO Plants from Plants has already begun populating playrooms and master builds across the world. Read more about these sustainable pieces in the following pages.

Plants from Plants tree branches on the assembly line.

In March 2019, when a whale was found dead in the Philippines with more than 80 pounds of plastic waste in its stomach, the incident confirmed some of biologists' worst fears concerning the amount of waste polluting Earth's oceans. In April, when another whale was found off the coast of Italy with a similar amount of plastic in its stomach, the issue's impact became even harder to ignore. According to *National Geographic*, 18 billion pounds of plastic waste enters the world's oceans from coastal regions every year, which they go on to point out is enough to pile five grocery bags of plastic on every foot of coastline in the world. As of January 2019, less than 5 percent of the world's plastic waste was recycled, leading to phenomena like the Great Pacific Garbage

Patch, a floating conglomeration of debris—much of it plastic—the size of a small continent.

As the problem becomes more apparent, however, governments and businesses are beginning to take action, with countries like Peru banning single-use plastics and cities like San Diego banning Styrofoam. According to the LEGO Group's VP of Environmental Responsibility Tim Brooks, however, the Denmark-based company has had plans in place to begin making their iconic product from bio-based, sustainable material for some time. "We will have fully sustainable bricks by 2030, but actually fully sustainable packaging by 2025," says Brooks. "We've really understood that the world wants us to move fast on packaging, and the world is challenged by packaging and plastic. We've been

reflecting that plastic is this fantastic material but it really shouldn't be used in single-use applications and then thrown away, so that's why we've changed our ambition on packaging."

He's not wrong. *National Geographic* claims much of the 40 percent of disposable plastic waste currently polluting our planet comes from packaging rather than products, meaning a large chunk of the plastics problem can be solved simply by changing how we pack consumer goods. The LEGO Group has been partnering with the World Wide Fund for Nature for more than five years, examining how best to create an experience that gives users exactly what they've come to expect from the LEGO System in Play while also being sustainable and producing no plastic waste. "Through [the WWF] we've already doubled down on our energy efficiency commitment."

The first step in this sustainability process came with something that makes intuitive sense, as well as being a savvy business move that allows the LEGO Group to test its bio-based sustainability goals in a compartmentalized piece of its manufacturing. Plants from Plants creates trees, leaves and other foliage for LEGO sets using real plant products. "[The WWF] runs an organization called the Bioplastic Feedstock Alliance, [and] they've helped us audit and understand where the material comes from: how it was grown," says Brooks. "Just because it was grown from plants doesn't mean it's a silver bullet. So that's where they've really helped guide us to ensure the material is as sustainable as it can be."

The process of finding exactly the right mixture of materials to create the perfect LEGO product from bio-based materials is an ongoing one, with Plants from Plants offering a unique opportunity to absorb some of the trial and error involved in the process. For example, the current material used in bricks and the bio-based materials used for things like leaves and dragon wings vary a great deal in terms of hardness. "We use about 20 different materials to make our pieces, and about 75 to 80 percent of our pieces now are made from ABS plastic, which is a quite rigid material," explains Brooks. "The sustainable material we've begun using is plant-based polyethylene, which is a more flexible material, and the sets you'd find that in are those that include pieces like dragon wings, plants, trees, bushes. It's important to see this as a journey—we started with polyethylene, but we also hope to find more sustainable materials for ABS plastic."

The goal for the LEGO Group is to offer a product that is completely sustainable while also being unrecognizable as different from the original. And early reactions to Plants from Plants show the goal is a reachable one. When the first Plants from Plants boxes came off the assembly lines, they were given away with purchases of $35 or more. "We wanted to get it [out] there and have people touch them and test them, and we're happy to say even our adult fans—who rightly hold us to account when things change—couldn't tell the difference. It's the same great quality, the same safety—it's just a more sustainable source."

LEGO Sustainable Superheroes at play among Plants from Plants elements.

ONE BOX, ONE GOAL, ENDLESS POSSIBILITY

What you get when you buy the LEGO Group's first green set.

In a creative preview to what LEGO fans can hope to find when the iconic brick becomes an entirely bio-based enterprise at some point in the 2020s, the 29-piece Plants from Plants giveaway set has inspired builders to create "sustainable superheroes," LEGO heroes whose primary building material can be found in the box. Not only do the heroes prove the feel of these new LEGO pieces is the same, it also shows just how important a green future has become for the LEGO Group and its fans alike.

According to the LEGO Group, 100 percent of the energy used to create LEGO bricks is "balanced by renewable energy generation in the form of wind power."

The safety in particular is of paramount concern for the LEGO Group as it continues to experiment with new materials. Their bricks have always been made to be cross-compatible, so a brand-new set will contain pieces that could fit together with the very first LEGO bricks, and their preestablished plastic materials made sure the bricks were always uniform and never brittle no matter how much they are used. Creating the perfect experience and maintaining the same standards is the main point of the material experimentation Brooks expects will continue until 2030. "Of course the molding is incredibly precise because the bricks need to be able to stick together to build a model but also easy enough to break apart so a child can pull a model to pieces—that's what we call 'clutch power,' and that's very difficult to get right," he says. "Even down to things like the sound: If you drop a bunch of bricks on the table it's a specific sound. There are many bio-based materials out there but they don't meet those criteria."

All of the trial and error is necessary for the LEGO Group, Brooks explains, because sustainably producing products and alleviating the glut of plastic waste currently engulfing our planet will ultimately create a world in which more children are free to learn from the LEGO System in Play. "What we're very passionate about is learning through play, which is this fantastic skill we want to bring to more kids across the world," continues Brooks. "When kids play, they learn. And when they learn, they develop. We realize our company vision is to inspire the builders of tomorrow. So if we somehow compromise children's future by making a product that damages the environment, we don't feel that's what a toy company should do. The world is running out of 'stuff,' as in materials, so how do we make sure we don't generate any waste in our production?"

In 2019, the LEGO Group was included in Reputation Institute's annual RepTrak 100 survey, making the top 10 in "most highly regarded companies in the world" for the ninth year in a row.

JPL/NASA

Three LEGO minifigures were sent aboard the *Juno* spacecraft by NASA representing the Roman god Jupiter, his wife Juno and scientist Galileo Galilei. *Juno* launched in August 2011 on a mission to gather information about the planet Jupiter.

LEGOstalgia

Some of the most beloved LEGO sets of all time still speak for themselves even after years of newer products have arrived.

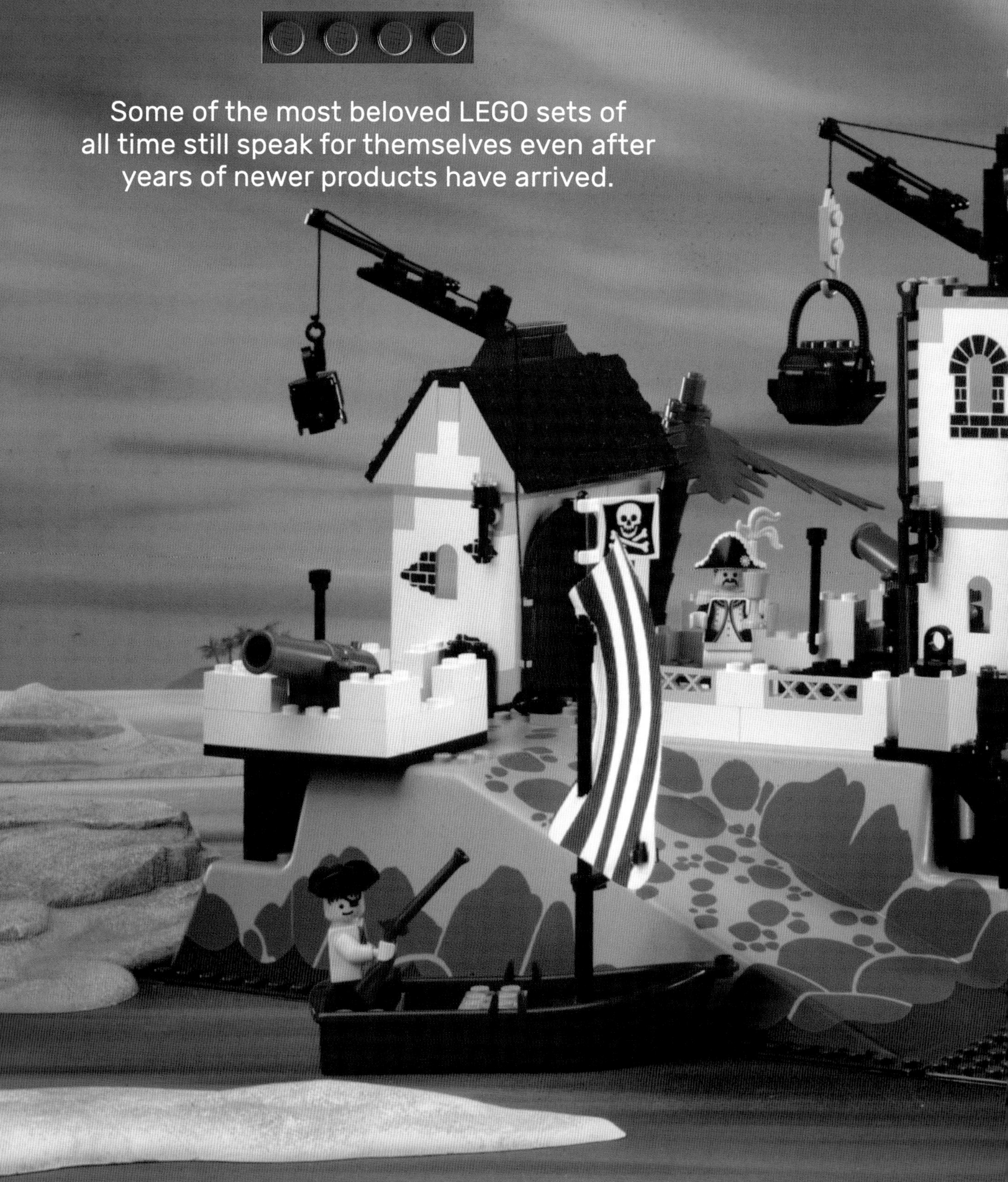

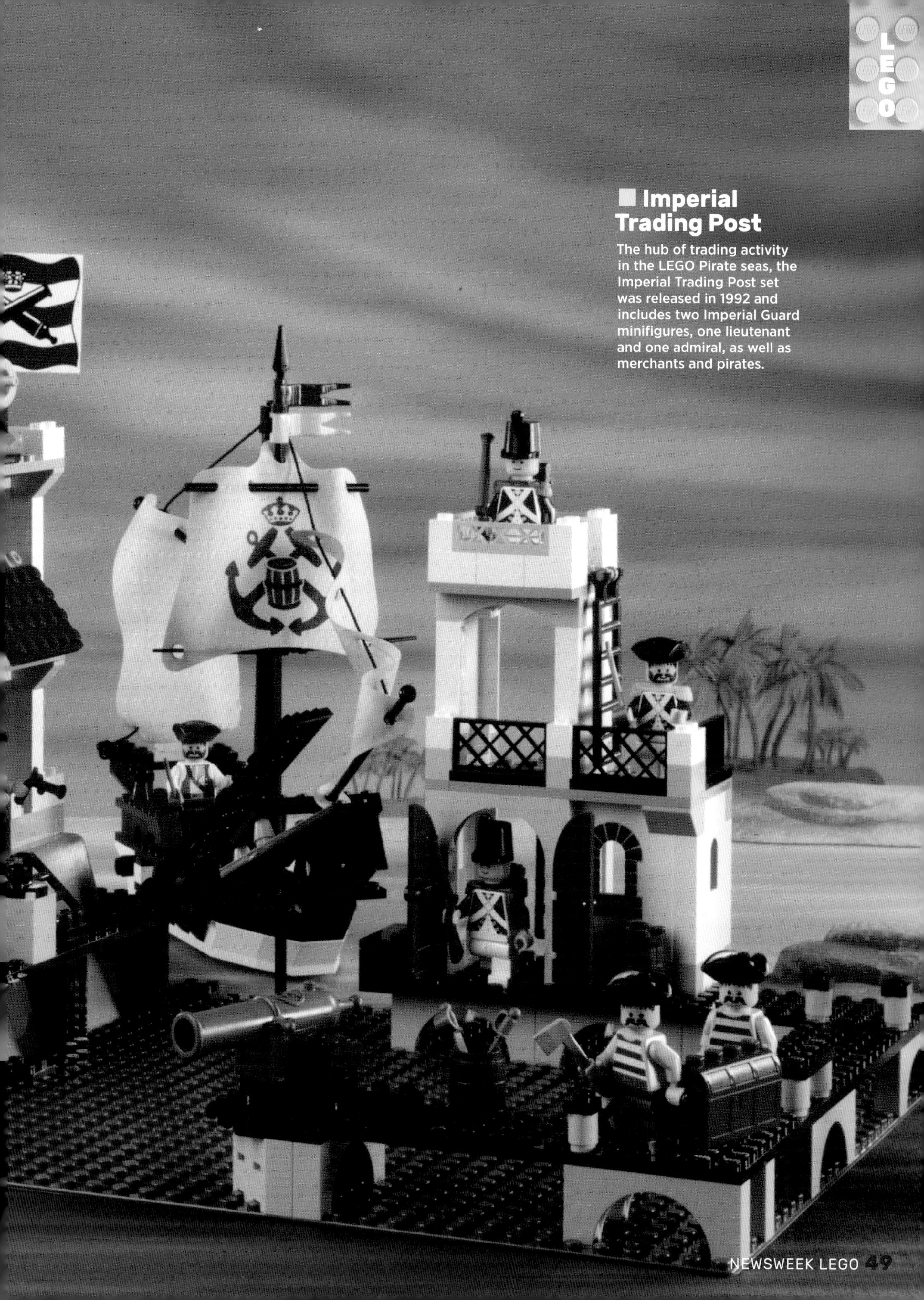

Imperial Trading Post

The hub of trading activity in the LEGO Pirate seas, the Imperial Trading Post set was released in 1992 and includes two Imperial Guard minifigures, one lieutenant and one admiral, as well as merchants and pirates.

Black Seas Barracuda

A classic pirate brig with two masts and a Jolly Roger flying, the Black Seas Barracuda has been among the icons of LEGO Pirates since its 1989 release.

Captain's Hold

Among the bricks included in the Black Seas Barracuda set are a number of gold coins, jeweled 1-by-1 bricks and golden goblets, as well as a map of the seas.

■ Forbidden Island

Part of the original run of pirate-themed sets, Forbidden Island was a pirate hideout that included a boat, shark, cannon, treasure chest and three pirates (as well as an Imperial soldier). The set was a great ancillary addition to the theme.

Rock Island Refuge

Built on a baseplate with a central pit that serves as a pirate treasure trove, the Rock Island Refuge set also comes with a boat, but this time it belongs to Imperial troops, not pirates. It is a peaceful outpost that pirates have invaded and now protect.

Pirates Perilous Pitfall

When Captain Redbeard comes to this island hideaway in search of Imperial gold, it's up to the Imperial troops to keep the gold in their rightful hands, with the help of a booby trap hidden in the island's stone. The set was released in 1997 and came with three pirates, a conquistador skeleton and a crocodile.

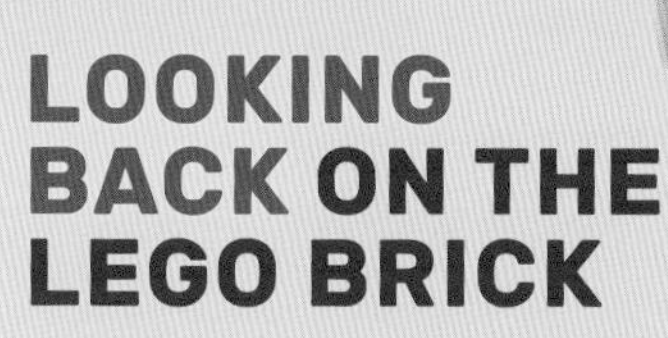

LOOKING BACK ON THE LEGO BRICK

Amy Corbett, Design Manager at the LEGO Group, revels in LEGO nostalgia every day at her job.

Do you remember the first LEGO set that inspired your imagination? What were the circumstances of this first encounter?
One of my earliest memories is playing with my brother and his new LEGO pirate ship. We would spend hours creating stories and using our brick box to build new worlds and adventures for them to go on.

I think that is one of the things about LEGO play that is so great—the universality that makes it so easy for people of all ages and genders to play together.

Are you surprised at the level to which the LEGO brick has permeated the culture? Why do you think it's so popular?
The LEGO brick itself has long been an icon. I think that's down to its simplicity as a stand-alone item, then the endless creative opportunities it has when combined with other LEGO bricks. That has allowed us to keep the same icon but continually refresh it over the years.

What is the greatest thing about working with the LEGO Group?
Having a passion for the brand definitely means going to work every day is something I actually look forward to. It's great to really believe in the products you are developing and work with so many other passionate and talented people.

If you had to pick just one LEGO set to show to someone with no knowledge of what LEGO bricks could do, which set would it be?
Having worked on the LEGO Disney line, I think I would have to pick something from that, like Cinderella's castle or Rapunzel's bedroom. The sets are full of cute details and story moments that take you right back to the movie and bring so much play. There is also so much nostalgia that will take any adult right back to childhood. And it's always so cool to see how you can use the bricks to recreate such iconic scenes and buildings.

Do you have a favorite product line or set? What is it about the set that makes it memorable for you?
I will always have a soft spot for LEGO Friends. It was the product line I was working on six years ago when I first started, so it's where I really learned to be a LEGO designer, creating my first sets and getting to know the bricks. But also because I know that if it had been around when I was a little girl, I would have loved it. It always brings out the inner child in me.

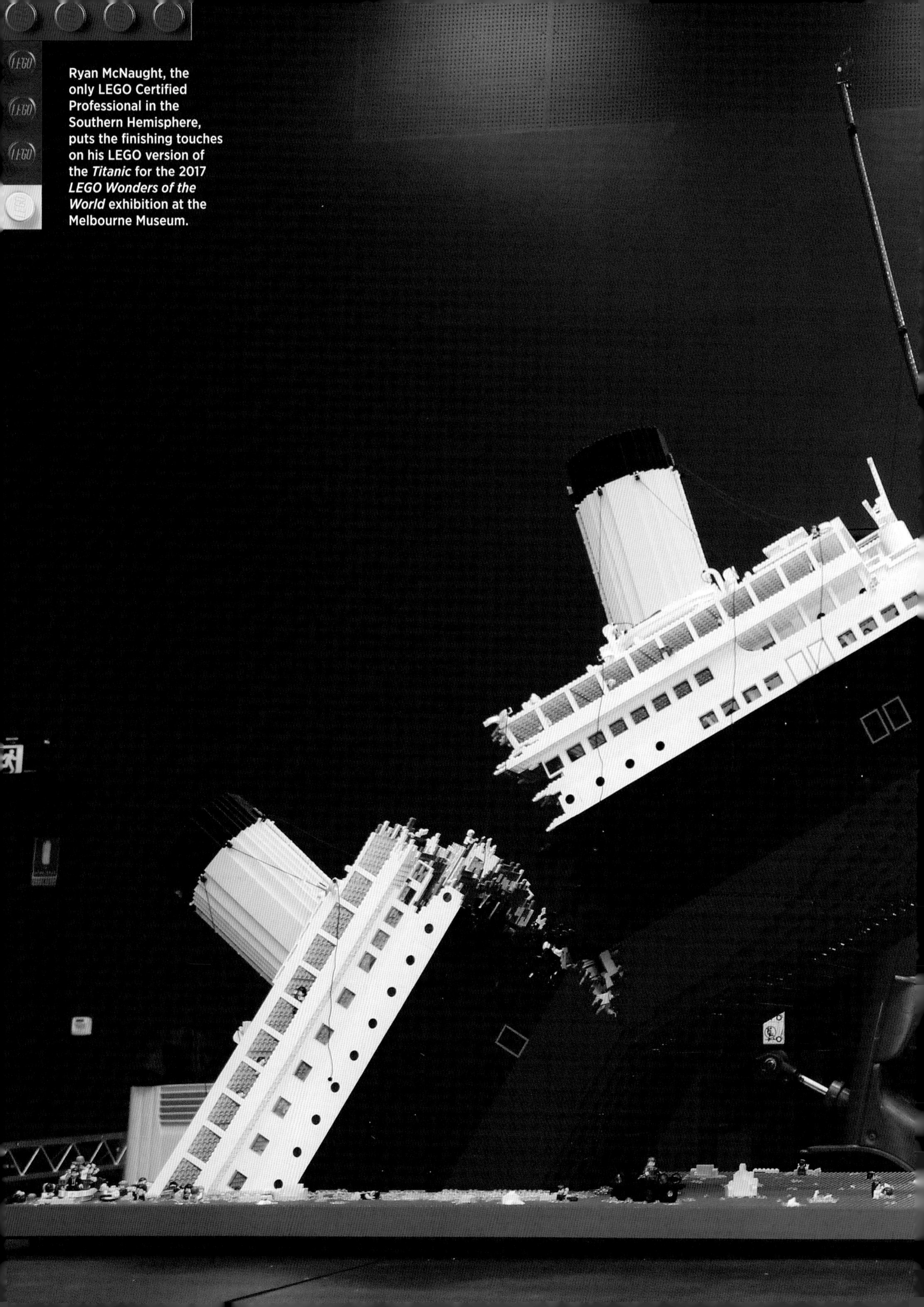

Ryan McNaught, the only LEGO Certified Professional in the Southern Hemisphere, puts the finishing touches on his LEGO version of the *Titanic* for the 2017 *LEGO Wonders of the World* exhibition at the Melbourne Museum.

Ryan
TOYOTA 20

Castle Set No. 375

One of the LEGO Group's first castle-themed sets, No. 375 included 14 knights, four horses and six 1-by-1 windows, marking the last time this measurement was used for windows in a LEGO set.

LEGO Knights

In the 1970s, the LEGO System in Play went Renaissance and had users practicing their siegecraft.

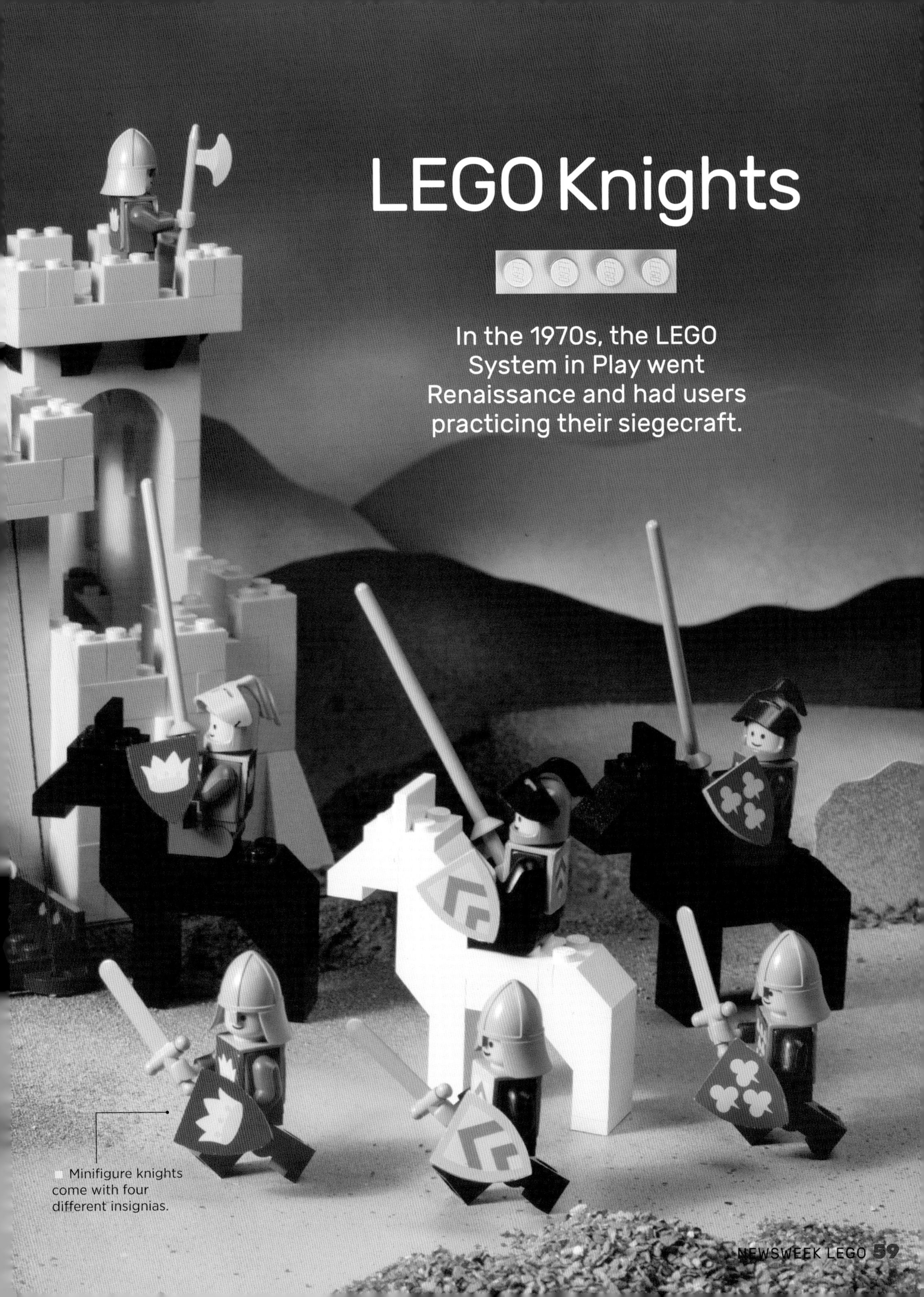

Minifigure knights come with four different insignias.

Knight's Castle

Released in 1984, this LEGO Castle Black Falcons set came with two more horses and six more knights to populate users' LEGO manor town. The 408-piece set originally sold for about $27.

A LEGO sign above the door lets passersby know there's refreshment here.

A minifigure innkeeper offers drinks.

Guarded Inn

Protected by a Crusader knight (on horseback) and two Crusader infantrymen, this roadside inn set was small at just under 250 pieces when it was released in 1986, but proved so popular it was rereleased in 2001.

■ Important spectators can watch from a royal tent.

■ Knight's Challenge

A jousting tournament makes a perfect centerpiece for a multi-set LEGO Castle build. Released in 1989, it saw the Crusader knights facing off against villains clad in black armor.

■ Horses included with this set come with wartime regalia.

■ A working drawbridge is included as part of the build.

Black Knight's Castle

Originally released as Dungeon Master's Castle, in 1994 the LEGO Group changed the name of this set, which comes with 12 minifigures and has a dungeon built into the base.

Fire Breathing Fortress

Home of the wizard Majisto, the Fire Breathing Fortress set was released in 1993 and came with knights, guards and a dragon. The second floor features a trapdoor that sends enemies straight down to the dungeon.

Guards armed with bows and crossbows protect the tower.

Unlike the dragon featured in LEGO Vikings, this dragon is molded plastic rather than LEGO bricks.

LOOKING BACK ON THE LEGO BRICK

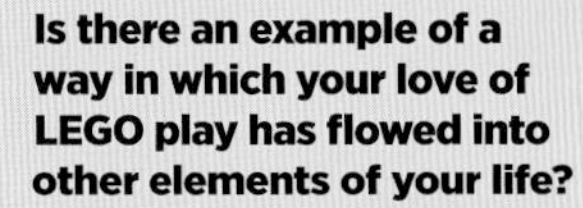

Kristian Reimer Hauge, Culture Mediator at the LEGO Group, is steeped in literal tons of LEGO history.

What's it like working with the entire history of the LEGO brick every day?
Working in the historical department of the LEGO Group, we sometimes need to create new exhibitions. This means building a lot of LEGO sets for display, not just recent ones but also older sets, which can be both fantastic and frustrating. It is a dream come true to build classics from scratch, but at the same time you really get to appreciate the work your colleagues in the building instructions team are doing. I can tell you that our building instructions have come a long way in the last 30 to 40 years!

How many sets are we talking about?
We have a lot of very large product archives in the historical department. One of these archives is called the vault and is a basement filled with almost all retail LEGO sets from the mid 1960s until today. One of my privileges as a culture mediator is that I sometimes get to show visitors the vault and, even though I have done it many times, it is always amazing to see the look in people's eyes when they suddenly find themselves holding the set they got for their 7th birthday or for Christmas. The memories and emotions these sets evoke is something I never get tired of being a part of.

Is there an example of a way in which your love of LEGO play has flowed into other elements of your life?
I use it as a kind of therapy from time to time. We all know life can be stressful and sometimes you just need a break from what's on your mind. When I feel stressed, I turn to LEGO bricks. This is one of the best ways for me to clear my mind. I am not a hugely skilled builder, so when I build with LEGO bricks, I must focus on the task at hand.

If you had to pick just one LEGO set to show to someone with no knowledge of what LEGO bricks could do, which set would it be?
I know this may sound tacky but honestly, it doesn't matter. It is not a question of what specific set you get in your hands. It is a matter of getting LEGO bricks, any LEGO bricks, in your hands as this is how you learn what they can do. You will instantly start to try and put them together. Having never had LEGO bricks in your hands before, it might take you a while to put them together in a satisfactory way, so you iterate. You build something...take it apart again...build something new in a different way.... You experiment, explore and learn along the way.

One Small Step for LEGO Bricks

Launch Pad

Built into the side of a crater, the 1978 LEGO Launch Pad was a 170-piece set that included a launch tower and control center, three astronauts, a rocket and a ground transport with a trailer for space samples.

Command Centre

The 1978 LEGO Command Centre, part of the Space theme, was not sold in the U.S., where the nearly identical set No. 493 Space Command Center was in stores instead, leading to an interesting situation for modern collectors. The set consisted of two rovers, four astronauts and a base station.

Galaxy Explorer

Containing a spaceship, landing pad with tower, four classic space Minifigures and a moon rover, set #928 (1979) featured a ship's cockpit big enough for two astronauts. This exact set was not released in the U.S., but the identical 497 Galaxy Explorer was put on shelves. Both sets, however, featured the No. 928 on the side of the spacecraft.

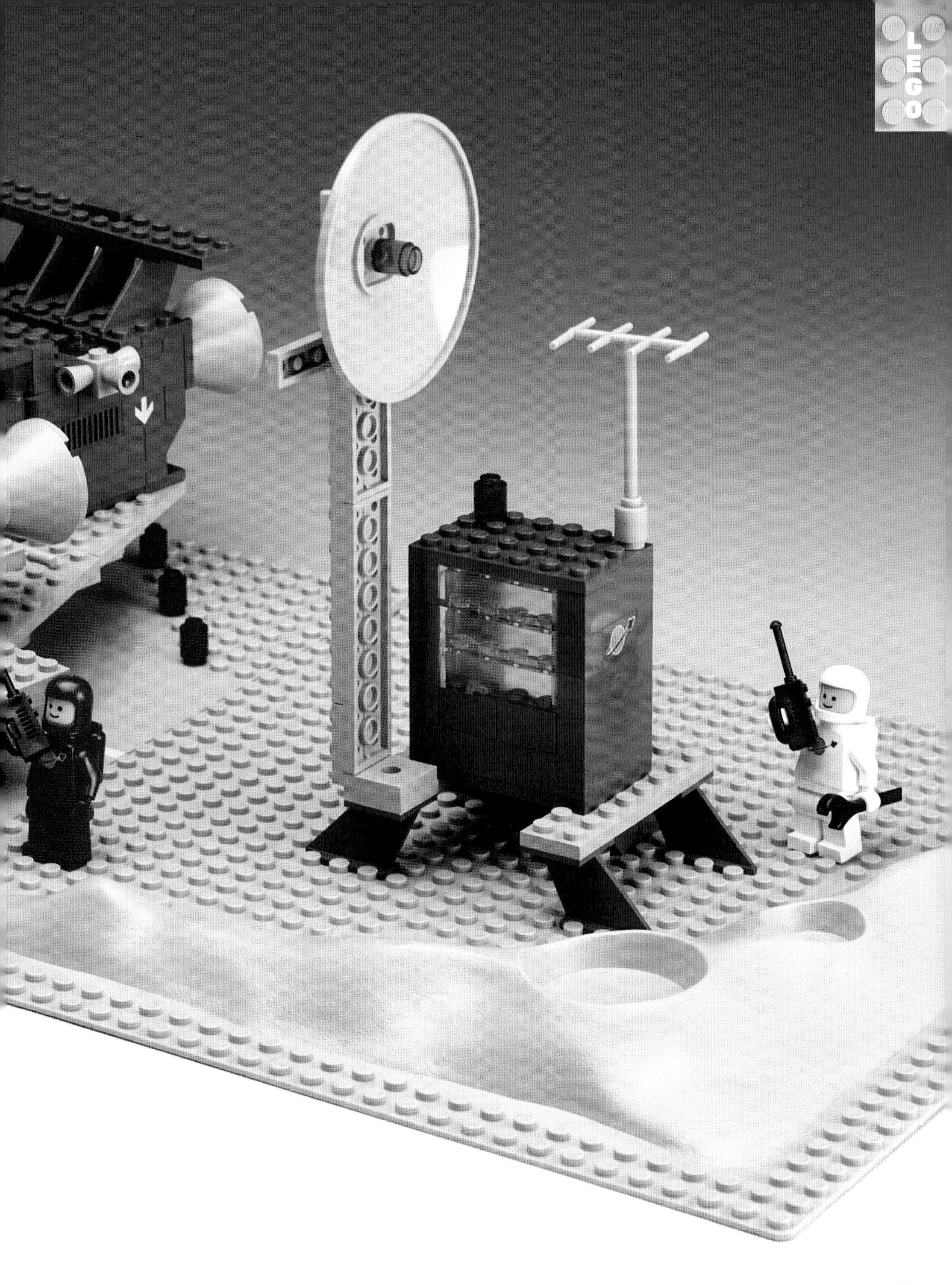
LEGO

Beta-1 Command Base

Another surface station on a foreign world, 1980's Beta-1 Command Base was a futuristic, modular set that included a monorail track, spacecraft, rover and astronauts to man them. It could also be built along several different lines, pictured here and opposite at top, as well as in the box art, inset above.

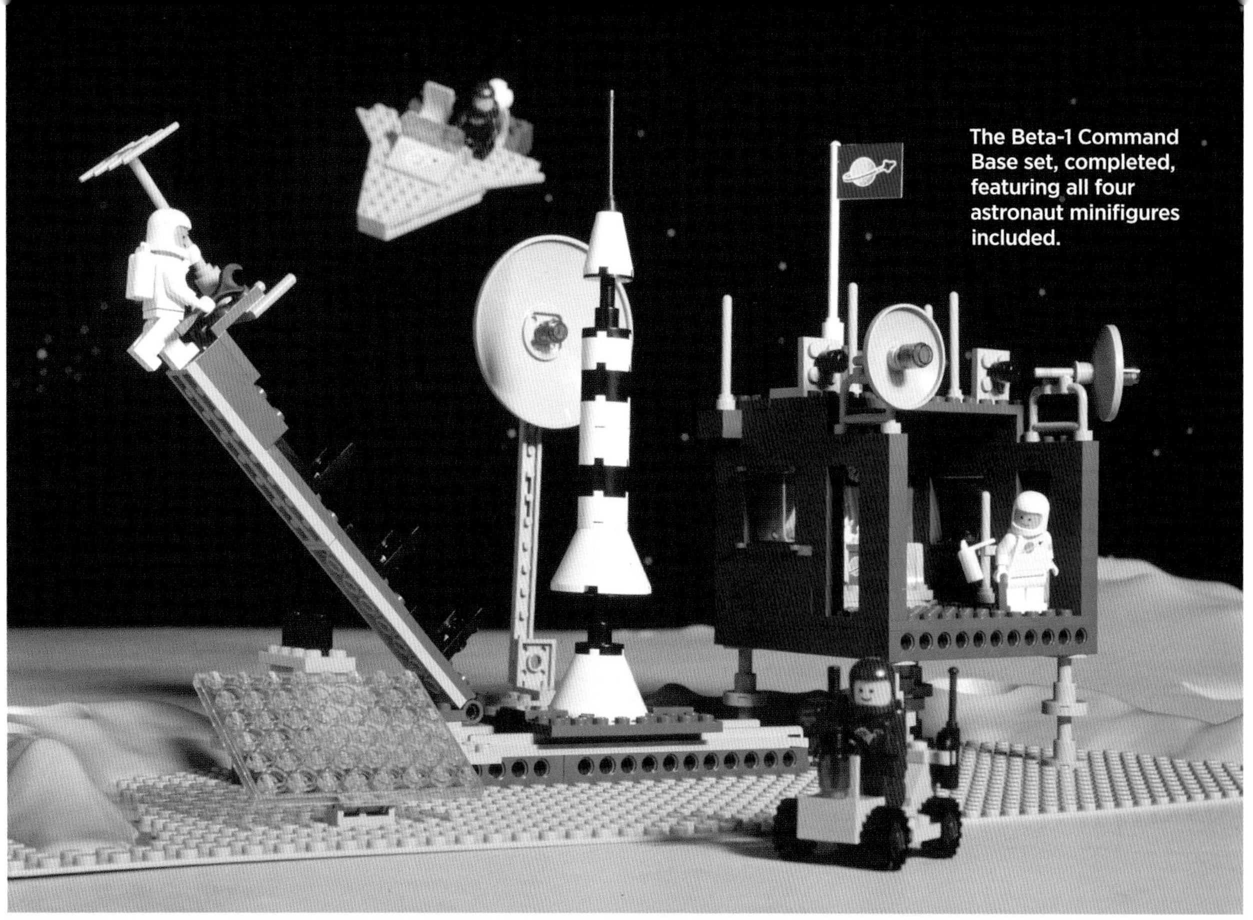

The Beta-1 Command Base set, completed, featuring all four astronaut minifigures included.

Space Supply Station

When 1983's update on the space station theme came around, hovercraft were included along with the usual rovers and astronauts.

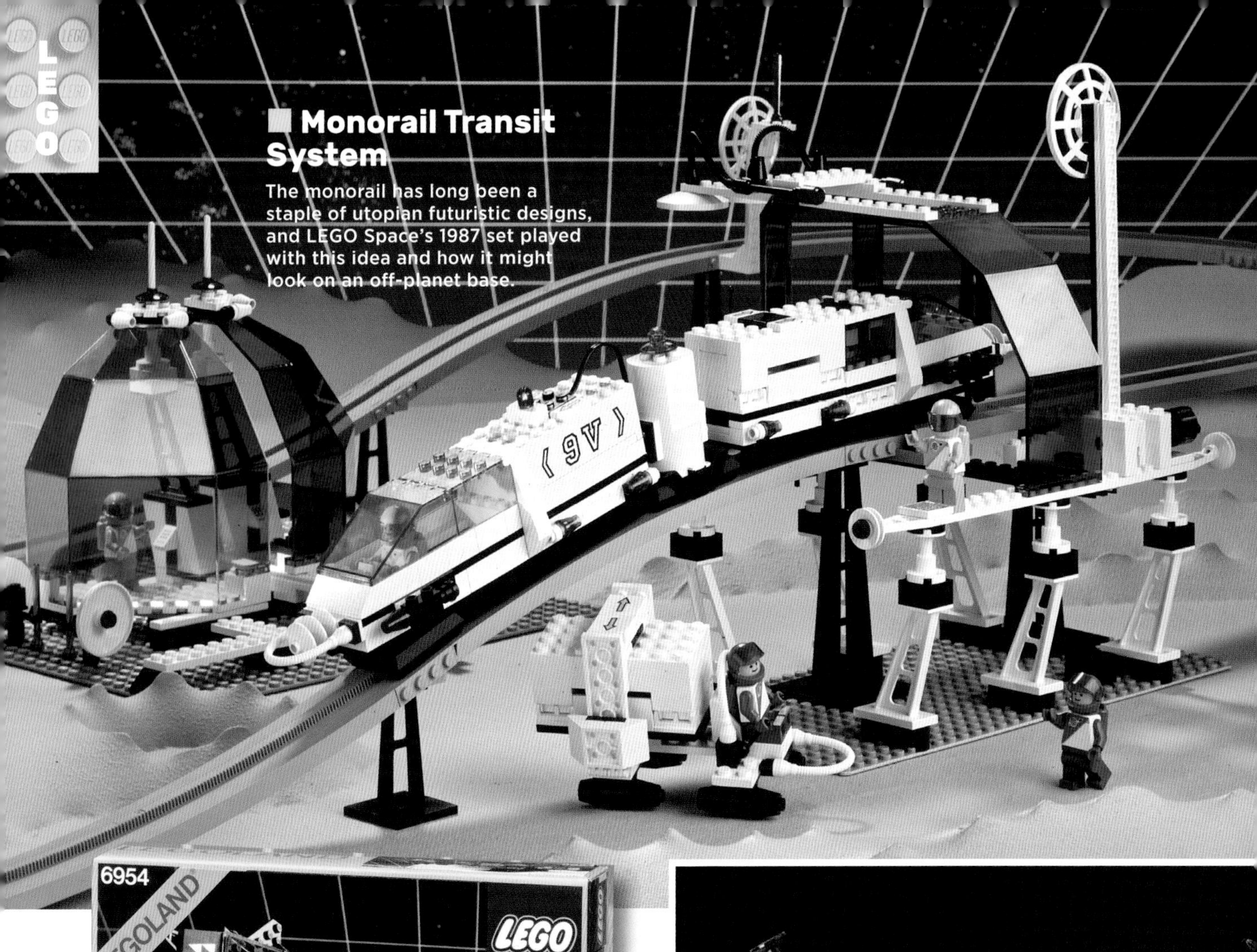

Monorail Transit System

The monorail has long been a staple of utopian futuristic designs, and LEGO Space's 1987 set played with this idea and how it might look on an off-planet base.

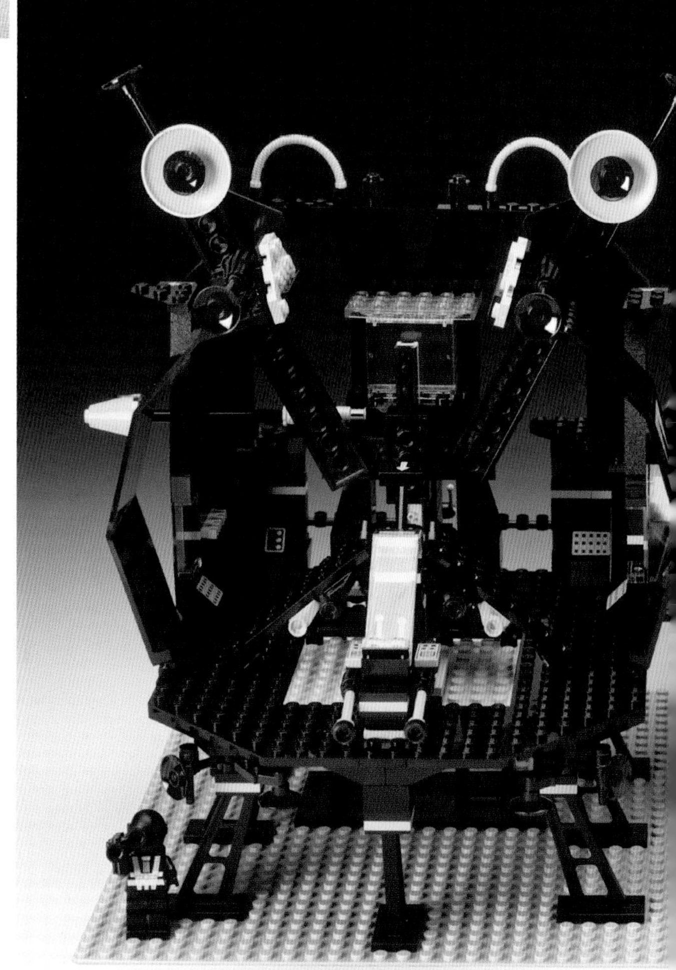

Renegade

By the late 1980s, LEGO Space had divided into two factions, the Blacktron and the Futuron. The Renegade, a 302-piece spaceship, was the largest in the original Blacktron fleet.

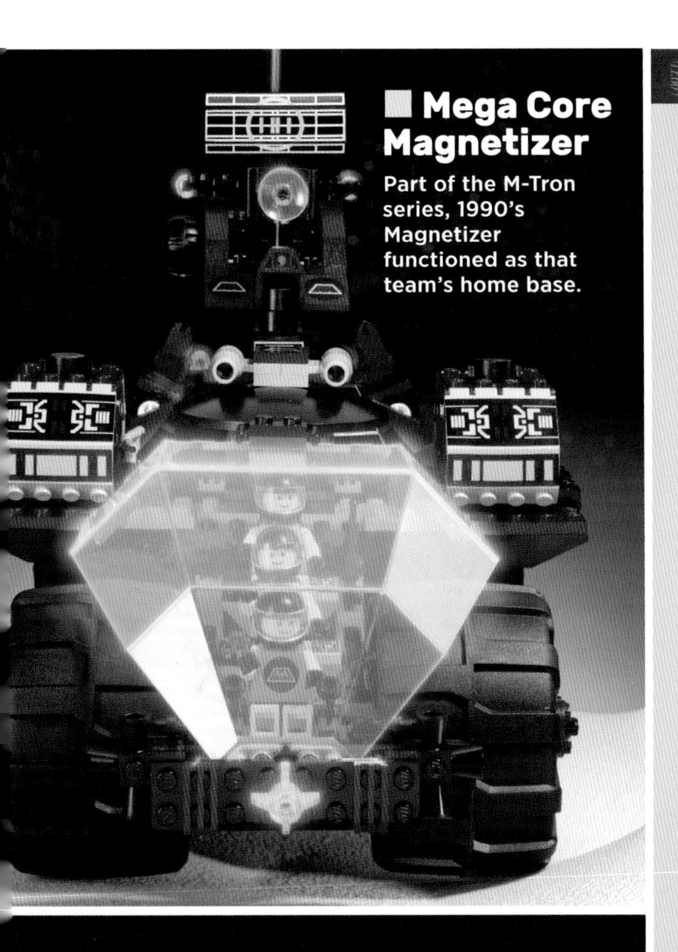

Mega Core Magnetizer

Part of the M-Tron series, 1990's Magnetizer functioned as that team's home base.

Message Intercept Base

Another Blacktron set consisted of a Blacktron outpost and a small spacecraft for taking scouts abroad.

LOOKING BACK ON THE LEGO BRICK

William Thorogood, Vice President of Innovation at the LEGO Group, derives inspiration from a lifetime of LEGO memories.

Do you remember the first LEGO set that inspired your imagination?
I have played with LEGO sets for as long as I can remember and still have the DUPLO trains from the 1980s that I played with before that. The first set that I vividly remember getting and being fascinated with, however, was handed down to me by my older cousin: LEGO 8846 Tow Truck, an early Technic model packed with functionality that absolutely fascinated me trying to understand how things worked.

How does that passion carry over into your everyday work at the LEGO Group?
The LEGO brand values are held in very high regard at the company and really do translate to everything we do. Imagination, of course, is essential when working to shape the future of play. Creativity [is] necessary to bring that imagination to life in a way that people can experience firsthand. Fun—well, if a toy isn't fun to make, then it will never really be fun for a child to play with! Learning: In 15 years at the LEGO Group, I don't think I have ever had the same day twice. We are constantly evolving, adapting and learning to become better at what we do. Caring: Of course, when working in early innovation projects there can be a lot of uncertainty and a lot of ideas that don't make it. I have to make sure to care for the people I work with and give them the support and coaching needed to constantly stay ahead of children's expectations. Quality: Growing up with LEGO bricks around me and even then understanding how important the quality of this system was, it has to be a part of what we do to deliver the best quality experiences to children around the world and pass on the feelings of happiness I had back when I was playing on my parents living room floor 30 years ago.

Has your experience with the LEGO System in Play carried over into any other areas of your life?
My love of LEGO play from an early age has really revolved around the ability to tinker and experiment with the bricks to bring my ideas to life. As a child, it was the only accessible means for me to do so, but growing up I find myself using that same tinkering mentality around the home, making things for the garden, customizing my cars and even clothing. LEGO play has always encouraged me to learn by doing and I will continue to do that throughout my life.

LEGO
POLICE

City Beginnings

LEGO City has been reflecting our real world in bricks for decades.

■ The LEGO Police Headquarters' jail features latticed windows. Bars wouldn't be introduced until 1996.

1979 Police Headquarters

LEGOLAND Town's 1979 police station set reflected how far the popularity of minifigures had taken the brand. Vehicles were now big enough to fit minifigures inside and the uniforms got an update.

1985 Airport

LEGOLAND Town's Airport was a 530-piece set, a behemoth for its time, and featured a control tower, terminal, runways, a plane and helicopter combo, and all the minifigures necessary for making the hub run. Inset: A minifigure porter helps a minifigure passenger with his check-in bags.

The gray 1-by-1 tile made a handy burger box.

1983 Hamburger Stand

LEGOLAND Town's Hamburger Stand featured a chef minifigure that could also be found on LEGOLAND's Main Street as a popcorn vendor, as well as working shutters for closing time.

1987 Emergency Treatment Center

LEGOLAND Town only produced a few medical-themed sets, but this EMT center is among the most remembered. It had two stretchers that doubled as hospital beds, orderly and doctor minifigures and even a LEGO brick ambulance. Inside the building were an operating theater, recovery ward and welcome center.

LOOKING BACK ON THE LEGO BRICK

"THERE'S something wonderful about the City aesthetic that gets to the essence of what something is. In its simplest form, it's a car or a police station or a firehouse and that's something that takes me back to my childhood. The actual structures are a very clean, simple aesthetic. By using these larger pieces and creating this cleaner look, it gives kids that are new to the building system a good entry. It allows them to have the confidence that they can build and handle the pieces and create something that looks very clean and modern. The city is wonderful: It has a purity to the design that I think is unique. Then, once [those kids] gain that confidence, the beauty of the Creator line is that you can add details, go back to the old world and add some new details. The clean, blank slate evolves into other recognizable aesthetics. For example, when we're working with our carmaker partners, the lines of a car are extremely important... you have to get the curves right for people to buy into it. But we tell them when we meet with them that we're not making a die-cast model of their car, we're incorporating their aesthetic into our building system."

—Jamie Berard, Design Manager Specialist, the LEGO Group

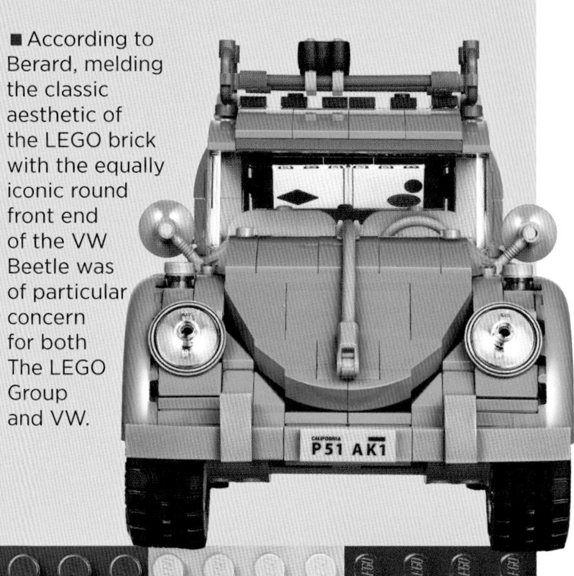

■ According to Berard, melding the classic aesthetic of the LEGO brick with the equally iconic round front end of the VW Beetle was of particular concern for both The LEGO Group and VW.

Emerald Night

Released in 2009, this old-fashioned train set is a testament to everything that LEGO bricks have become to fans since the Castle set opened up a universe of possibilities. In set #10194 (the number also appears on the engine's door), the train is a combination of classic LEGO brand aesthetics and the imaginative possibilities presented by LEGO Ideas and a generation of builders who have been building with LEGO bricks since childhood.

LEGO Norse Fantasia

LEGO Vikings imagined a world of warriors, heroes and dragons.

■ The longship's oarsmen wear the same black glitter helms that appear in the other LEGO Vikings sets.

■ This LEGO Viking Catapult came in a set with the Nidhogg Dragon.

■ Viking Ship Challenges the Midgard Serpent

Including six minifigures to man it and totaling more than 500 pieces, the 2005 Viking Ship Challenges the Midgard Serpent set was based on the shape of the Viking longships that set out to find places like Iceland, Greenland and Newfoundland.

Viking Warrior Challenges the Fenris Wolf

The largest part of this 2005 Vikings set is the brick-built wolf that threatens a minifigure armed with an ax, sword and shield.

Thanks to a loot chest and clear green bricks, the fortress could hoard emeralds.

Viking Fortress Against the Fafnir Dragon

The centerpiece of the Vikings theme, this fortress set includes a full-grown dragon, a baby dragon, catapults and other armaments. LEGO Design Master Bjarke Lykke Madsen is quoted in the book *Great LEGO Sets* as saying inspiration for the set came from Danish ring fortresses of the Viking Age.

The Viking fortress set comes with two different kinds of catapults: a large, heavily armored one that throws rocks and a smaller one that throws repurposed gray minifigure head elements.

LEGO Living

LEGO bricks are used to build a lot, but most of our first building experiences were with versions of what we know best: our houses.

"When I was young, I was always using LEGO [bricks] to build houses [rather than] cars.... Now that I have children, I can give them my old LEGO bricks and share that with them."

—NELLEKE VAN DER PUIL, VICE PRESIDENT OF MATERIALS, THE LEGO GROUP

Home Is Where the LEGO Bricks Are

Clockwise from bottom left: LEGO Town's classic Vacation Hideaway set, released in 1990; 2009's LEGO Creator Family Home could be built according to three different plans; the LEGO Town Plan from 1958 includes a hotel, gas station and houses; the LEGO Creator Modular Modern Home includes an electric car and solar panels. Any of these sets can now be adorned by collectors with plants made from actual plant matter, thanks to the efforts of Nelleke Van Der Puil and her team. To learn more about what the LEGO Group is doing to create a more sustainable future, turn to page 6.

Taj Mahal

LEGO Advanced Models shot the moon with its brick version of Agra, India's famous tomb.

A 5,923-Brick Masterpiece

Back in 2008 when Taj Mahal was first launched (Set no. 10189), it was the largest model with a piece count of 5,922. In 2017 a new version was introduced with 5,923 pieces (Set no. 10256). That gives one an idea of exactly how detailed the (pictured) updated 2017 set is, with its tiny pieces lending accents like windows made with 1-by-1 plates and a trademark onion dome made by stacking plate pieces. Featuring elements and colors that are rare in the LEGO universe and requiring odd techniques like the sideways building method needed for creating the blue rim that runs along the mausoleum's bottom, the set is an advanced builder's ideal.

■ The Taj Mahal set is hollow, which gives builders the option of placing a light inside.

Artist of the Brick

Nathan Sawaya has opened the door to LEGO bricks being taken seriously as a sculpting medium. He sat with *Newsweek* to introduce his art as well as what the LEGO brick means to him.

Nathan Sawaya poses with part of the Superman component of his latest exhibition, which features DC characters. Inset: Sawaya's famous Yellow, Green and Blue.

"If someone sees a marble statue, they can appreciate it, but when they come, it is unlikely they will have a marble slab they can chip away at. But when kids see art made out of LEGO bricks, they can be inspired, and go home and create with their own bricks."

How did you first get inspired to work with LEGO bricks?
Back when I was a lawyer and contemplating leaving the practice to become a full-time artist, I was reading a book about sculptor Tom Friedman's art. Friedman uses household items to create fantastic works of sculpture. Items like toothpicks or plastic cups are transformed into amazing art. His work inspired me to explore using LEGO bricks.

What benefits do LEGO bricks give sculptors?
I choose to use LEGO bricks for my medium because it makes the art very accessible. Families who may have never been to an art gallery were drawn to my exhibition, *The Art of the Brick*, because of that familiarity with the toy. They can connect with the art on a different level because they have played with the toy before. It's about the democratizing of the art world. Creating art out of this medium opens up the doors to the art world for more people. If someone sees a marble statue, they can appreciate it, but when they come, it is unlikely they will have a marble slab they can chip away at. But when kids see art made out of LEGO bricks, they can be inspired, and go home and create with their own bricks.

Is there anything about the aesthetics of the finished product that you don't get with other materials?
There is something amazing about LEGO bricks when used to sculpt large forms because up close the viewer is looking at tiny rectangles full of sharp corners and right angles. But then, when the viewer steps back, all those corners blend together, and the sculpture's shape comes into view. The right angles become curves, and instead of distinct lines, the viewer sees a human figure. As in life, it is all about perspective.

An early Batman comic cover from Detective Comics takes the shape of the caped crusader himself in Siwaya's work.

MICHEL GINIES/SIPA/SHUTTERSTOCK

The Art of the Brick: DC Super Heroes features Siwaya's takes on classic DC heroes like The Flash.

"I like to plan out the sculpture as much as possible. I visualize the final piece before I put down that first brick."

Much of your work is based on pre-existing art. How do you go about choosing your subjects?

I wanted to choose a broad selection of works both geographically and historically that also would be fairly recognizable and then reinterpret them using LEGO bricks. By interpreting past masters' works out of LEGO bricks, it presents a way to introduce art history to younger kids. How would you talk to a 5-year-old about the Mona Lisa?

How often are you building?

In my art studio, I generally have two to three different projects always going on. When I am not traveling with *The Art of the Brick*, I spend six days a week in the studio, working full days on the various art projects. I spend 10 to 12 hours a day in my art studio.

A life-size human form sculpture can take me up to two to three weeks. I have approximately 7 million bricks in my art studio in Los Angeles. They are sorted by shape and color in clear plastic containers. That way, when I am working on a project, I can immediately grab the bricks I need to keep building.

When I find inspiration for a new work of art, I'm always excited, but the next step is serious planning. I like to plan out the sculpture as much as possible. I visualize the final piece before I put down that first brick. As I am building I do glue each brick together. Because we ship artwork all over the world, I found that it is important to affix all of the bricks together to survive the shipping process.

But because I'm gluing the bricks, I sometimes have to use a chisel and hammer to break the bricks apart if I make a mistake. It can make for a slow process.

The Art of the Brick: DC Super Heroes is Sawaya's current exhibition, most recently at the Espace Chapiteau in Paris.

MANHATTAN HELP TEAM
FIRE
EHOUSE · 75

The LEGO Ghostbusters Firehouse Headquarters building set is photographed in 2015 before its release in New York, in front of the location from the film.

The Idea Books

From the 1960s to the 1990s, the LEGO Group provided inspiration to its builders with Idea Books like the one below, showcasing a world of possibilities.

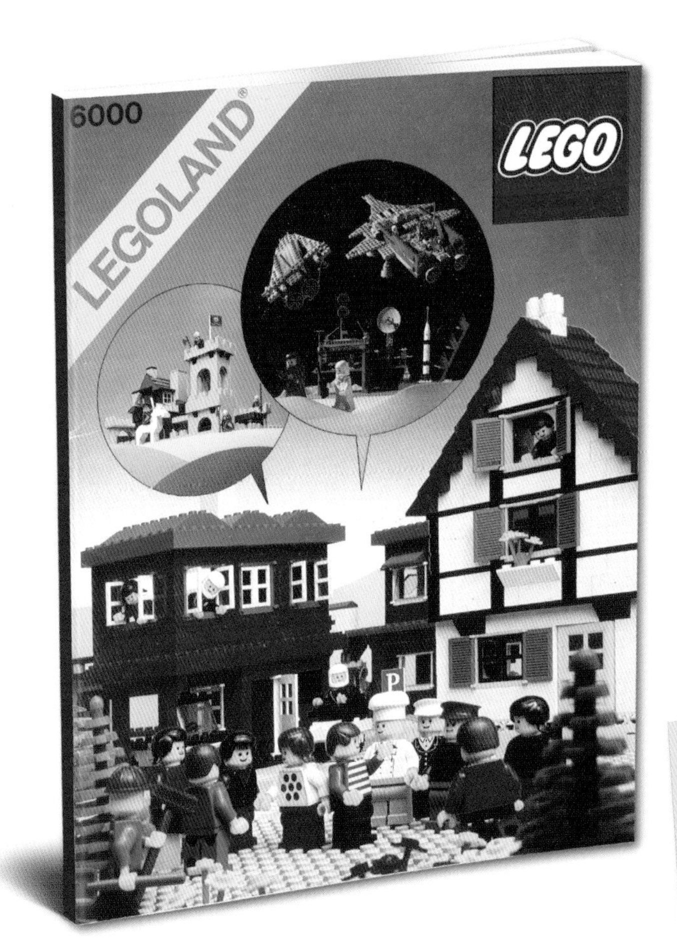

The LEGOLAND Idea Book

Released in 1980, the *LEGOLAND Idea Book* was ostensibly about the adventures of Bill and Mary, its main minifigure characters. But the real stars of the show were the builds constituting Bill and Mary's house and hometown. The couple first builds their LEGO house, then embark on a journey that takes them to a windmill, an airport, through downtown and to the movies.

Blasting Off

After their terrestrial activities, Bill and Mary take their classic LEGO spaceship to a space station on the moon. The elaborate build includes a launching pad for orbital rockets, space station workers and equipment, communications arrays and multiple starships.

The Beatles Yellow Submarine

LEGO designer Justin Ramsden and LEGO fan designer Kevin Szeto created the 15th product in the LEGO Ideas series as a tribute to one of the most iconic pieces of animation of all time. When *Yellow Submarine* premiered in 1968, it was immediately recognized as the vanguard of the psychedelic movement, and even down to the Fab Four's outfits, the set, released in 2016, is pitch perfect.

LEGO Ideas

The LEGO brick may have started as a plaything for children, but it has evolved into an inspiration for all ages.

THE LEGO SYSTEM IN PLAY gained worldwide notoriety as a tool that allowed children to build and populate their own worlds. But as the original LEGO fans aged (without aging out of their love of the LEGO Group) and the iconic brick found use as part of branded partnerships like Star Wars and Harry Potter, it became clear to every fan from Billund to Beijing that the LEGO System in Play was just as valuable an escape for adults as it was a tool for children.

According to the LEGO Group's Tormod Askildsen, Head of Adult Fans of LEGO: "Buying and building the sets is an escape and a relaxing way to create—a meditative outlet. The more people use the system, the more they master the components. They can begin realizing that any object can be recreated with LEGO bricks, [no matter the origin]. It's been a great way for builders to show off their talents as well as inspire the company."

It's in this spirit that the LEGO Group created the LEGO Ideas platform. This forum allows adult fans of LEGO—known internally as AFOLs—to share ideas for builds. The LEGO Group can then, in turn, look into creating actual LEGO sets based on the whimsy of its most dedicated fans. These builds run the gamut of pop culture, history and abstract constructs and have directly led to the creation of sets such as The Beatles' Yellow Submarine, NASA's Saturn V rocket and even a ship in a bottle. The result is a more democratic experience for users and a direct line to their hard core of fanatics to keep a finger on the pulse of trends. From rock stars to science milestones to brick birds that would make even the most ardent *Audubon* reader do a double take, that goal has been met and surpassed.

■ NASA Apollo Saturn V

LEGO builders Valérie Roche (aka Whatsuptoday) and Felix Stiessen (aka Saabfan) embarked on a particularly ambitious project for a 2017 LEGO Ideas release: The Apollo program's Saturn V rocket. Featuring exactly 1,969 pieces as a tribute to the year astronauts walked on the moon, the set features three removable rocket stages, a lunar orbiter and lunar lander. The set measures more than 39″ (100cm) high and 6″ (17cm) in diameter.

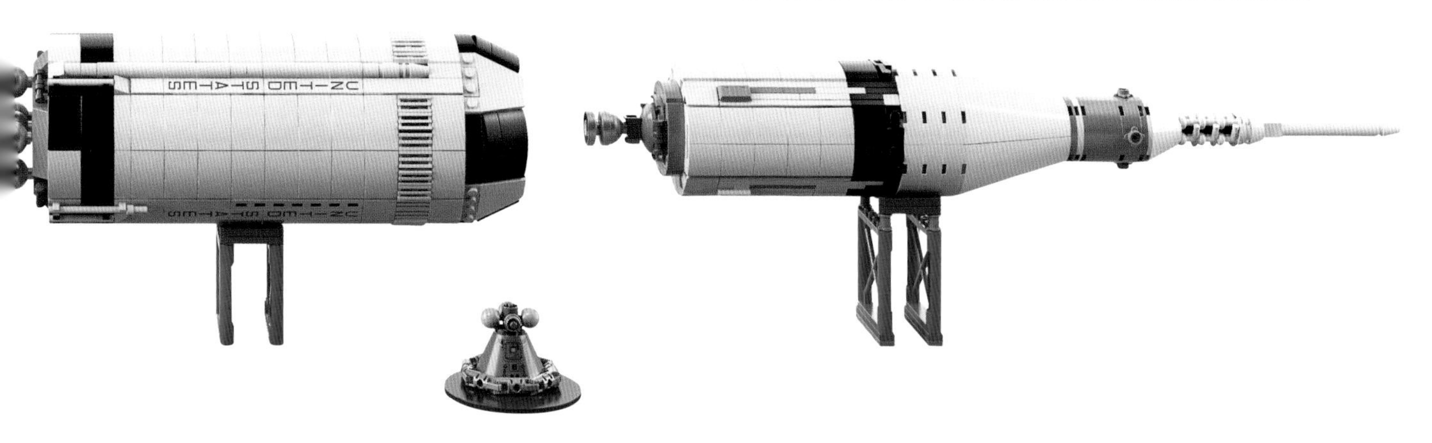

Ship in a Bottle

Designed by fan creator Jake Sadovich from Idaho, this LEGO Ship in a Bottle features all the hallmarks of both a traditional ship in a bottle and a classic LEGO set. Featuring 280 translucent-blue "water" elements, a ship with three masts and six cannons, and even a wax seal style element, the *Leviathan*, was an instant classic.

Exo Suit

This set features the astronauts Pete, Yve and their robot turtle on a quest in deep space for the mythical exo suit. An homage to classic sci-fi designs, the suit itself was designed by LEGO builder Peter Reid and features "posable limbs, opening cockpit, grabbing claws and an intricate, modular form." It also features Pete and Yve in their classic green spacesuits for the first time in three decades.

Birds

Created by LEGO enthusiast Thomas Poulsom, these three bird sets represent three different continents with the robin from Europe, the Blue Jay from North America and the hummingbird from South America. Featuring name plates that show the scientific name for each bird, these nature-inspired LEGO builds are unique as both playthings and showpieces.

■ Treehouse

With more than 3,000 pieces, this nostalgic piece from LEGO Ideas is a test for even the most dedicated AFOL. It features accessible cabins, a pulley winch system and interchangeable leaves so your treehouse can match the changing foliage of autumn.

Pop-Up Book

Acting like a real open-and-close pop-up book, this LEGO Ideas set, featuring more than 800 pieces, can live on a bookshelf or on open display. The classic Little Red Riding Hood theme makes it a timeless addition.

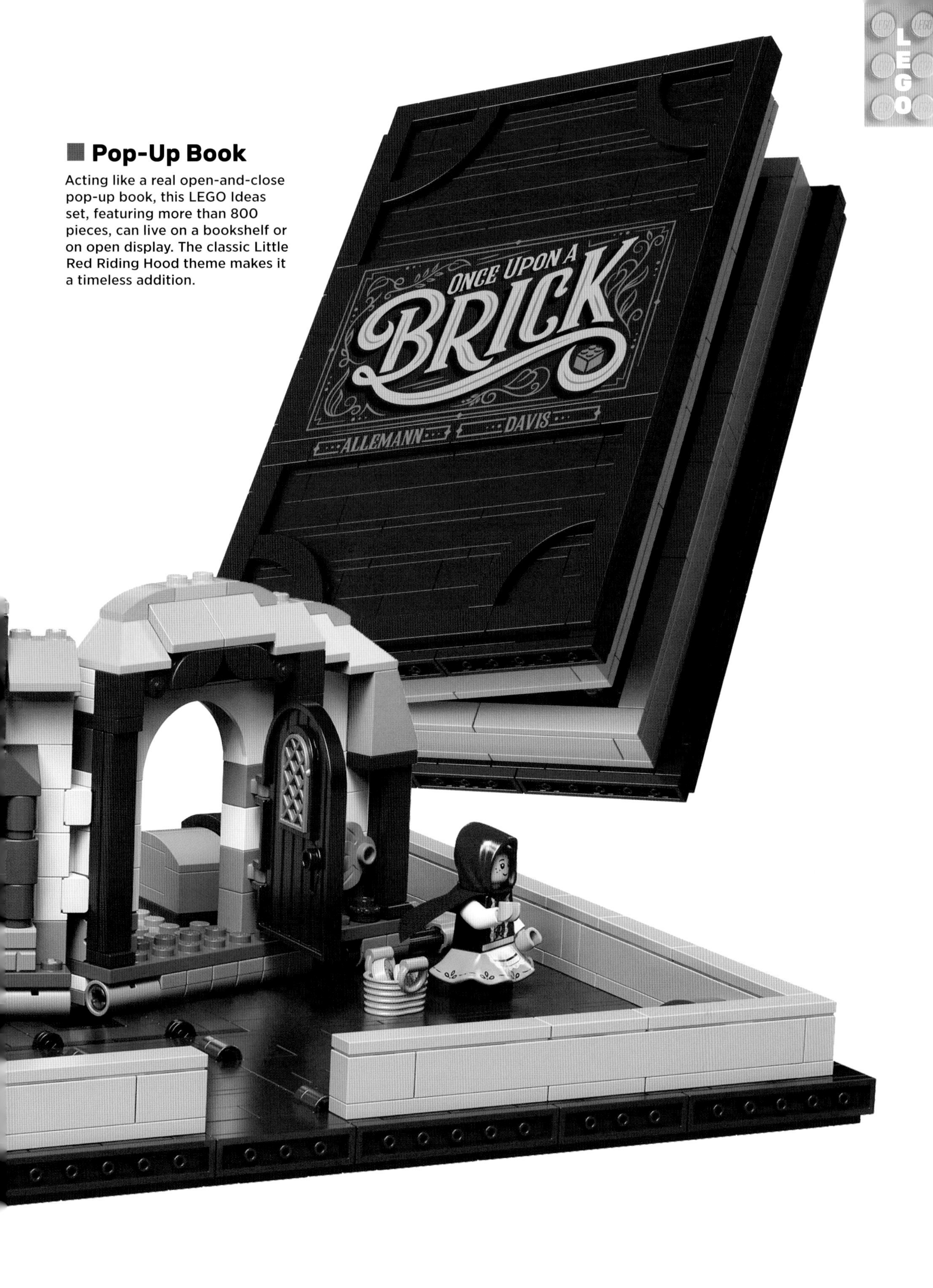

Naomie Harris, the James Bond franchise's current Miss Moneypenny, explores the intricate Aston Martin LEGO set inspired by the films.

Lunar New Year

■ Revelers enjoy a LEGO brick dim sum meal on a real rotating lazy susan.

For Chinese New Year 2020, LEGO brought its celebratory sets to the world.

■ Traditional dragon puppets were recreated in LEGO brick.

■ Dragon boats add to the traditional feel while offering depth to the set.

■ The set comes complete with BBQ stalls and hawkers.

■ A Lunar New Year Celebration

After fans all over the world expressed their interest in a 2019 Lunar New Year set sold exclusively in China, for 2020 the LEGO Group released the Chinese New Year Temple Fair set. This 1,664 piece cultural milestone celebrates the Year of the Rat with collectible minifigures and unique festival architecture. "Fu" decorations, "best wishes" scrolls, red envelopes and "paper" windmills add an authentic Chinese cultural touch while teaching younger builders about the traditions of Lunar New Year.

Niels B. Christiansen, CEO of the LEGO Group. The company was founded in 1932 in Denmark.

The LEGO Leader

Niels B. Christiansen, CEO of the LEGO Group, opens up to *Newsweek* about the experience of overseeing the company that helped shape his childhood.

Do you remember the first LEGO set that inspired your imagination?
As most Danish children, I played with LEGO bricks as a child. While I can't really recall the first LEGO set I received, I have particularly fond memories of a set with a model of a LEGO house. It had these distinctive red windows and doors and, while it today may seem like a simple feature, I recall being fascinated by the fact that the windows and doors were able to open and close. This was new in the 1970s, and the memory of opening and closing them stays with me as something I found quite amazing and cool.

Were new LEGO sets often a part of your life?
Most often we did not get new LEGO sets as gifts—instead we inherited loose LEGO bricks from family members—which we turned into LEGO creations. I remember vividly building houses and garages and cars on our living room floor. I must give credit to my mother's patience for allowing it because the projects would sometimes extend across several weeks, where the houses grew into a small city on the floor before being disassembled and used in new projects.

How do those memories inform the work you do for the company now?
Having played with LEGO bricks as a child and having followed the LEGO Group closely in my professional career, I felt I knew the company quite well, but it has been an overwhelming and surprising experience to join the company and feel firsthand the passion and emotional connection that so many children, parents and fans around the world have with our brand, our products and the experiences we create.

I receive letters from children, parents and grandparents on a regular basis, sharing their stories of building and having fun with LEGO play—and giving advice on where and what we can improve.

It's incredibly inspiring and motivating for me, and I know that it's the same for thousands of my colleagues around the world. In that sense, it is a constant reminder of who our most important stakeholders are: children. It also reminds me why what we do is so important. We impact the lives of millions of children, and that means we have a huge responsibility in delivering the best experiences to children of today—just as the LEGO designers did back in the 1970s when they developed the cool windows and doors I loved so much.

What do you think makes a memorable LEGO set?
It has to be an amazing model to build naturally. It should showcase the ingenuity and possibilities of the LEGO System in Play. And it should resonate with a wide group of kids and fans around the world so that they can remember it with affection not just as children, but also when they grow up—just like I can.

Why do you think the fascination with the LEGO Building System has continued to grow over the decades?
I think the secret is having a simple idea that has unlimited potential and a firm dedication to keep innovating and developing on this. To this day, the core experience of LEGO play remains the LEGO brick and the LEGO system, but we continue to take that simple idea and we reinvent it every year to make it better and more relevant. In that way, LEGO play also bridges the gap between generations and can gather families around an activity that is engaging and fun for all—something I have experienced with my own children when they were young. This is what makes LEGO bricks more than just another toy. Something unique.

The Brick Barons

Since 1958, LEGO bricks have been conquering playrooms all over the world. The sheer numbers involved speak to their dominance.

18

Average number of bricks produced in every million that fail to conform to the LEGO Group's strict conformity guidelines, or 0.0018 percent.

7,541

Approximate number of pieces in the largest commercially available LEGO set, the Millennium Falcon.

62

Years the original LEGO mold shape has been in use.

5

Number of times the LEGO bricks produced in a year could circle the circumference of the globe.

114

Height, in feet, of the world's tallest LEGO tower, built in Milan, Italy, in 2015.

80

Approximate number of LEGO bricks on Earth for each human resident.

700

Number of tires, in millions, produced each year by the LEGO Group, making them one of the world's largest manufacturers.

915,103,765

Number of possible combinations when connecting six eight-studded LEGO bricks.

4

Number of LEGO minifigures, in billions, currently around the world. If they represented a real nation, that nation would be the world's most populous.

LEGO
GJ 10
GJ 14

In Billund, fans of the LEGO brick who take the LEGO Inside Tour are given a unique parting gift designed each year by Kjeld Kirk Kristiansen.

Inside a LEGO Factory

The one-of-a-kind experience offered by Billund's factory tour can inspire LEGO novices and lifelong fans alike, showing them the sheer enormity of the brickmaking process.

NOT YOUR average behind-the-scenes look at a factory floor, LEGO's Inside Tour, located at its factory in Billund, is a two-day experience that leads the LEGO brick's most passionate fans through the company's long and storied run as one of the foremost creators of playthings in the world. Each tour's fees include two nights at the LEGOLAND hotel, and one of the foremost attractions is a guided tour through Ole Kirk Kristiansen's home, where some of the oldest toys created by the LEGO Group are still on display. Visitors are then taken through the factory itself, where they watch the process of plastic pellets known as granulate being made into everything from minifigures to 1x1 bricks to giant DUPLO bricks. The Inside Tour is available a few times a year, typically between May and September, with tickets released on the LEGO Group website several months in advance.

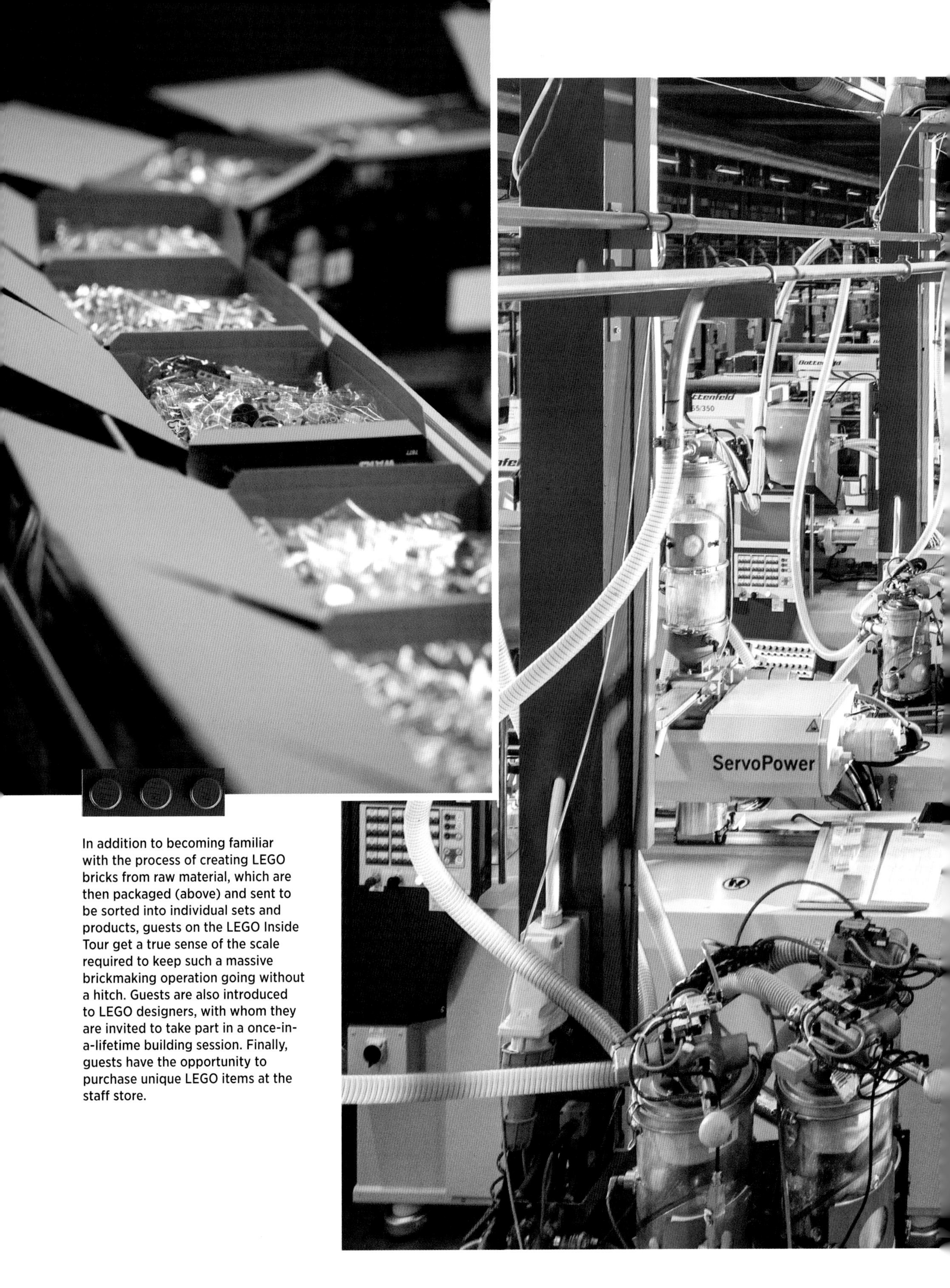

In addition to becoming familiar with the process of creating LEGO bricks from raw material, which are then packaged (above) and sent to be sorted into individual sets and products, guests on the LEGO Inside Tour get a true sense of the scale required to keep such a massive brickmaking operation going without a hitch. Guests are also introduced to LEGO designers, with whom they are invited to take part in a once-in-a-lifetime building session. Finally, guests have the opportunity to purchase unique LEGO items at the staff store.

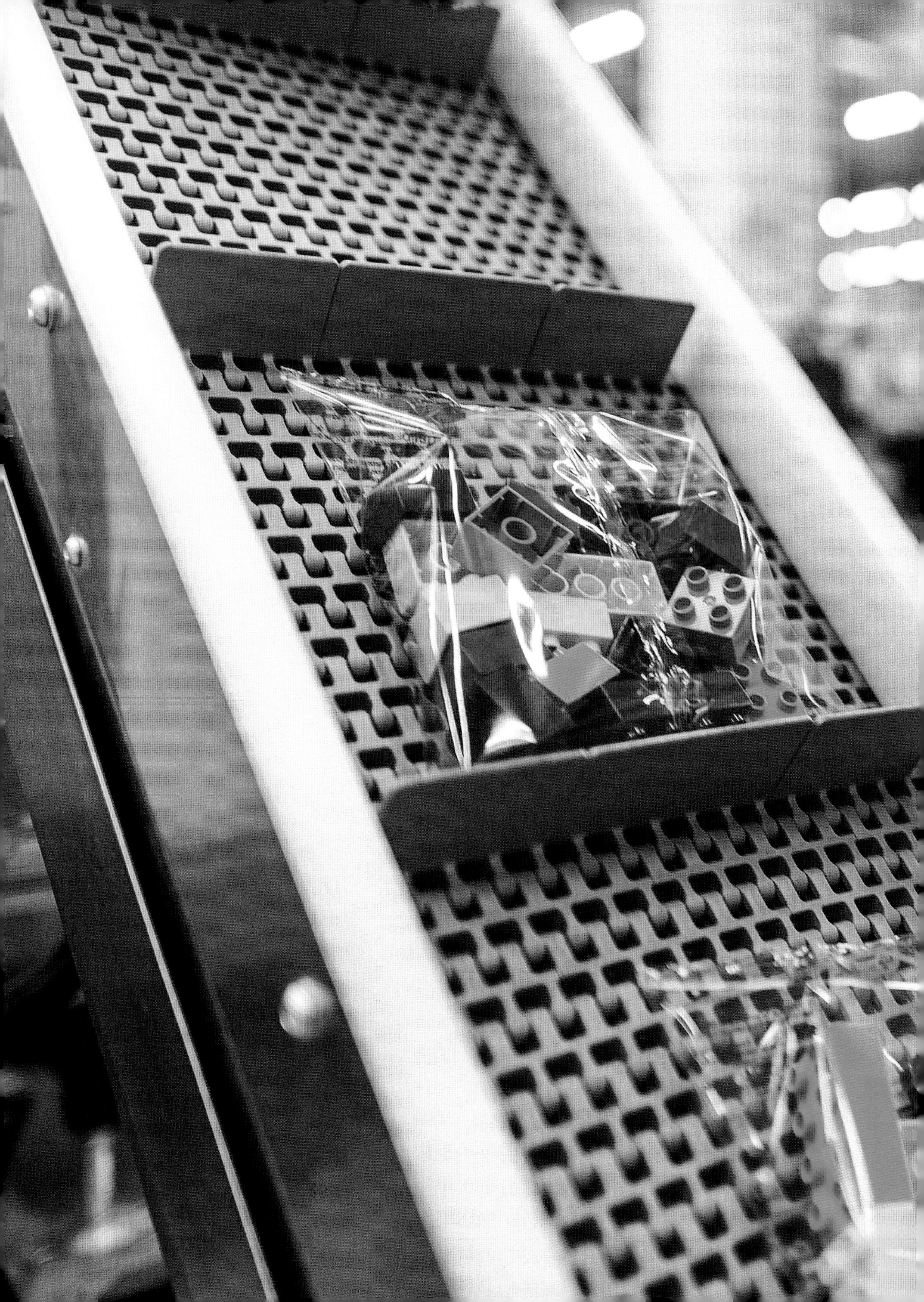

DUPLO bricks, the LEGO Group's early childhood line, are prepared for packaging. DUPLO bricks are double the height, width and depth of LEGO bricks to more easily fit smaller and less dextrous hands.

«LEGO® GARE, 5 M INUTES D'ARRÊT»

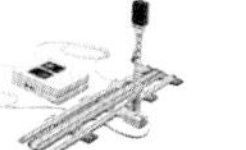

• Transformateur 12 V pour l'alimentation des locomotives, aiguillages télécommandés, signaux, et éclairages de la gare et des trains. (Réf. 7864) • Aiguillages électriques (Réf. 7856) et commande à distance (Réf. 7863). • Signal de commande lumineux (Réf. 7860) réglant la circulation des trains.

TRAINS LEGO®: A CONSTRUIRE ET A CONDUIRE A PARTIR DE 6 ANS.

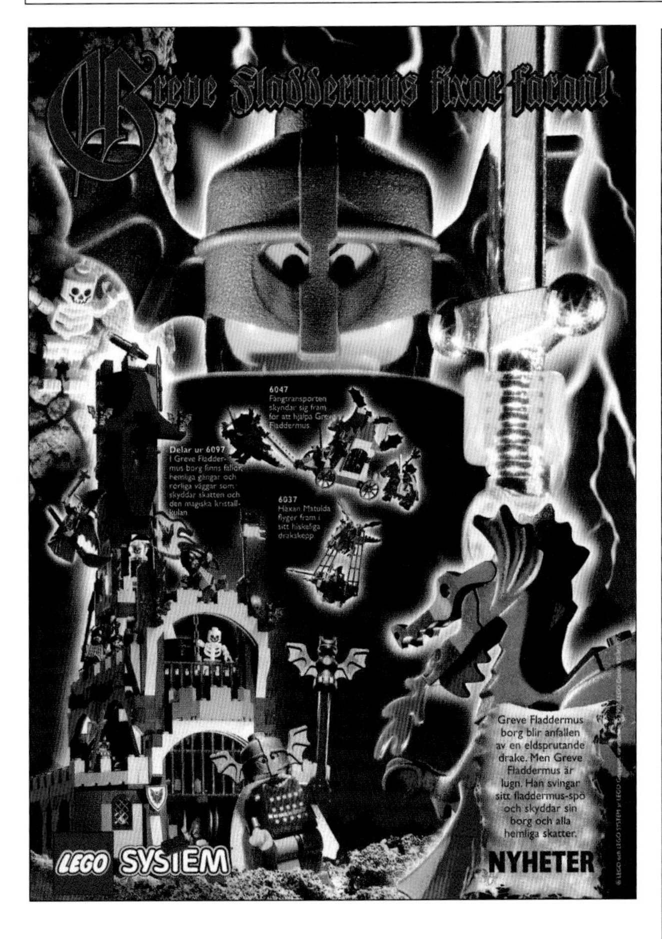

LEGO ads from throughout Europe, clockwise from top left: France, Sweden, Sweden, France, Italy and Sweden. In 2017, in the Nordic country's city of Gothenburg, the Älvsborg Bridge was painted to look like the pillars were made of LEGO bricks as part of the Let's Color Gothenburg initiative, which recruits unemployed local young people and trains them to become professional painters while working on public art installations.

NEW
FORCEFIELD AHEAD!
1.2.42
The new Space-ship is packed
packed with new exiting features: Colour scanners, holographic pictures, and a satelite disc. And all LEGO SYSTEM Space sets can be built and rebuilt into new exiting models. So stand by for transformation.
6854
Groundscan Vehicle.
LEGO SYSTEM
★ NEW
924814/96

LEGO LEGO レッツGOレゴ!! LEGO LEGO
海賊首領
南海の勇者
バトル・クイズ
©1988 LEGO Group
パチンパチンと止めるだけのレゴで、
こーんなビッグな海賊船が作れちゃった。
楽し〜いプレゼントつき!!
(85)

LEGO
LEGOLAND® Space
Galactic Jail Cruiser and Prisoner Transport are hunting 7 other new sets in LEGOLAND® Space right now.
"Get a free LEGO® Catalogue at your toy dealer."
6987
Blacktron Star Base
LIGHT & SOUND
6770
Magma Carrier with Flashing Lights & Siren
6932
Plasma-drive Starship
LEGO
6886
Space Police Hunter
921512

6986
Space Police Galactic Enforcer
6894
Blacktron Cruiser
6990
Space Trak Centre
6781
Space Police Prisoner Transport
6941
3 section Blacktron Prowler
6831
Space Police Patrol
6703
6 Spacemen
1.2.34 A
® The names LEGO and LEGOLAND are registered trade marks. © 1989 LEGO Group. 921512.

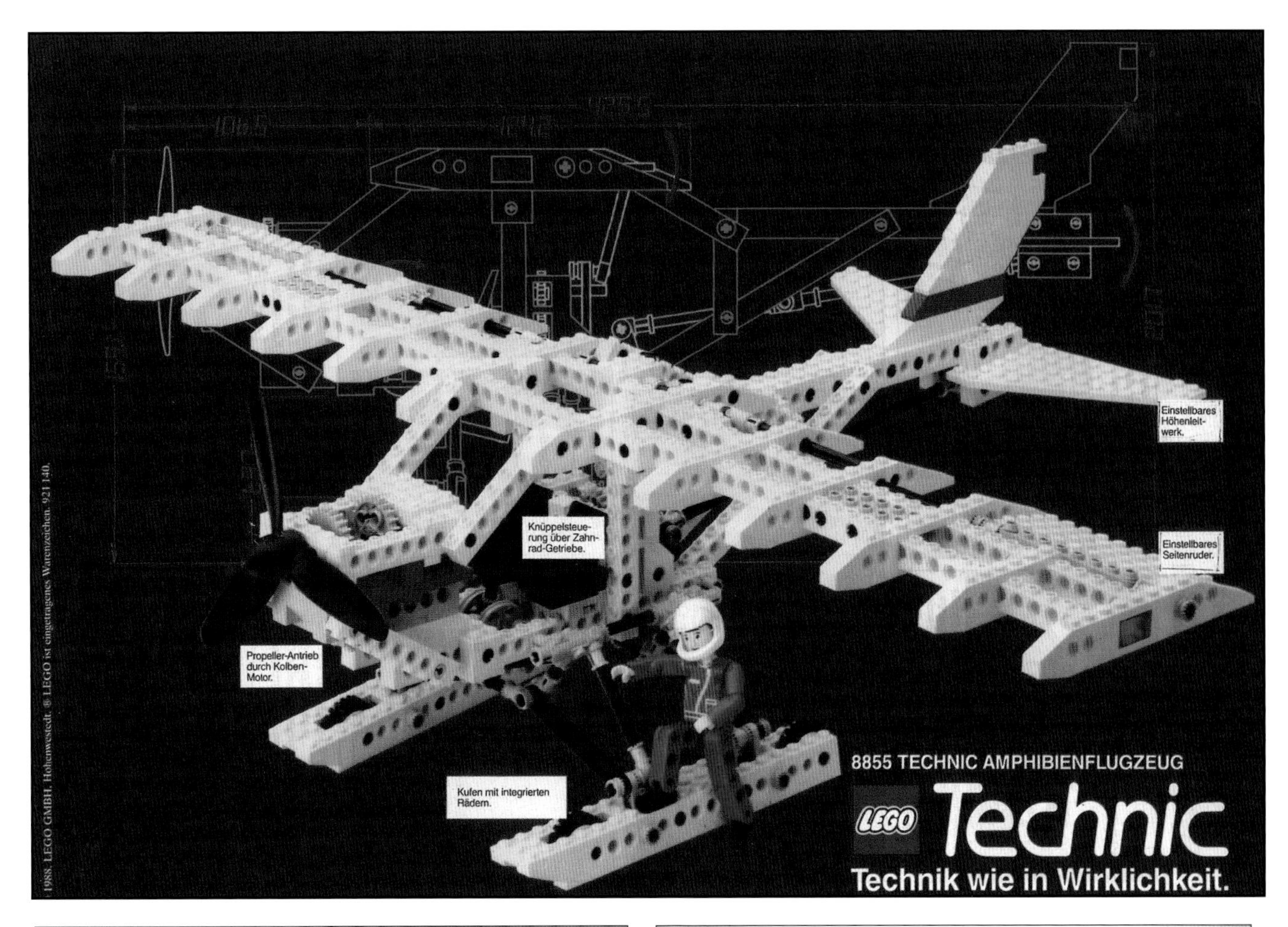

LEGO®
Un coup bien réfléchi.

LEGO®
Een verstandige zet.

Vous êtes assiégé de toute part et vous devez vous défendre âprement. Pour résister à ces attaques, vous devez faire confiance aux produits qui, preuve à l'appui, se sont avérés solides comme le roc depuis des années, qui se vendent facilement et régulièrement, qui ne vous encombrent pas de stocks superflus et qui se renouvellent chaque année. Comme LEGO® par exemple. Celui qui a misé sur LEGO peut être confiant et sûr de son affaire. Jour après jour, les boîtes LEGO passent sur votre comptoir. Depuis des années. Malgré la forte concurrence.

Avec LEGO®,
personne ne vous met échec et mat.

Ads depicting LEGO Pirates, Space, Technic, Paradise and a LEGO chess set show the variety of The LEGO Group's marketing efforts throughout the decades. The LEGO Group's earliest origins date back to a Danish family factory with 10 employees.

The Many Worlds of the LEGO Brick

With the benefit of many branded tie-ins, the LEGO brick continues to receive makeovers with every new set.

LEGO

Harry Potter

LEGO bricks found a fantastical new forum in 2001 when the LEGO Group began producing Harry Potter-themed sets and minifigures. Creating new sets on and off since then, the wizarding world has become a favored LEGO set choice for millions, from Privet Drive to the whimsy of Hogwarts. Sets featuring the wizarding school, the Whomping Willow and the Weasley Ford Anglia were released in 2018.

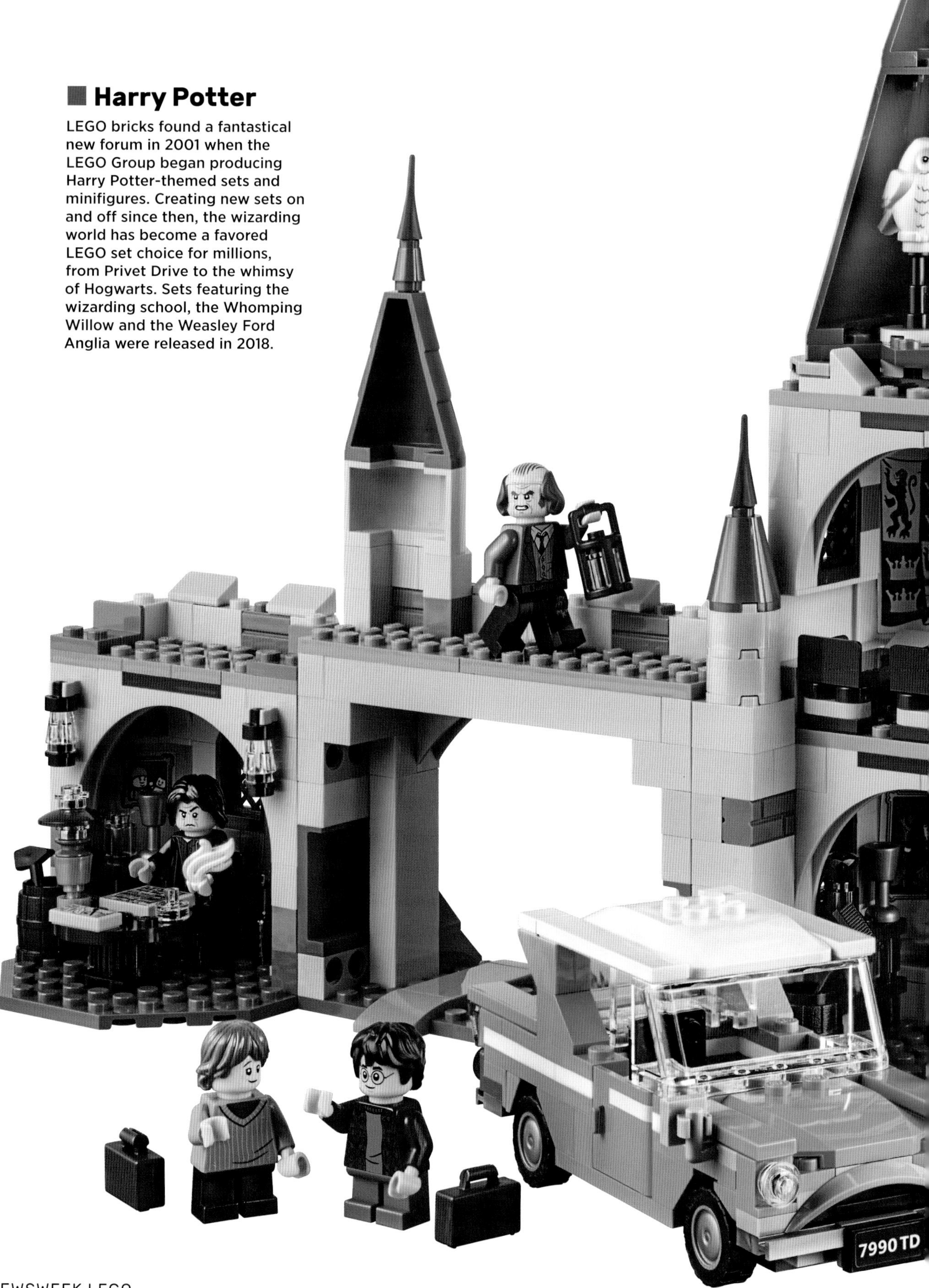

LEGO

Grindelwald's Escape

In the first set to be released in conjunction with the second installment of the *Fantastic Beasts* franchise, *The Crimes of Grindelwald*, minifigures representing Gellert Grindelwald and Seraphina Picquery duel in front of Grindelwald's escape carriage.

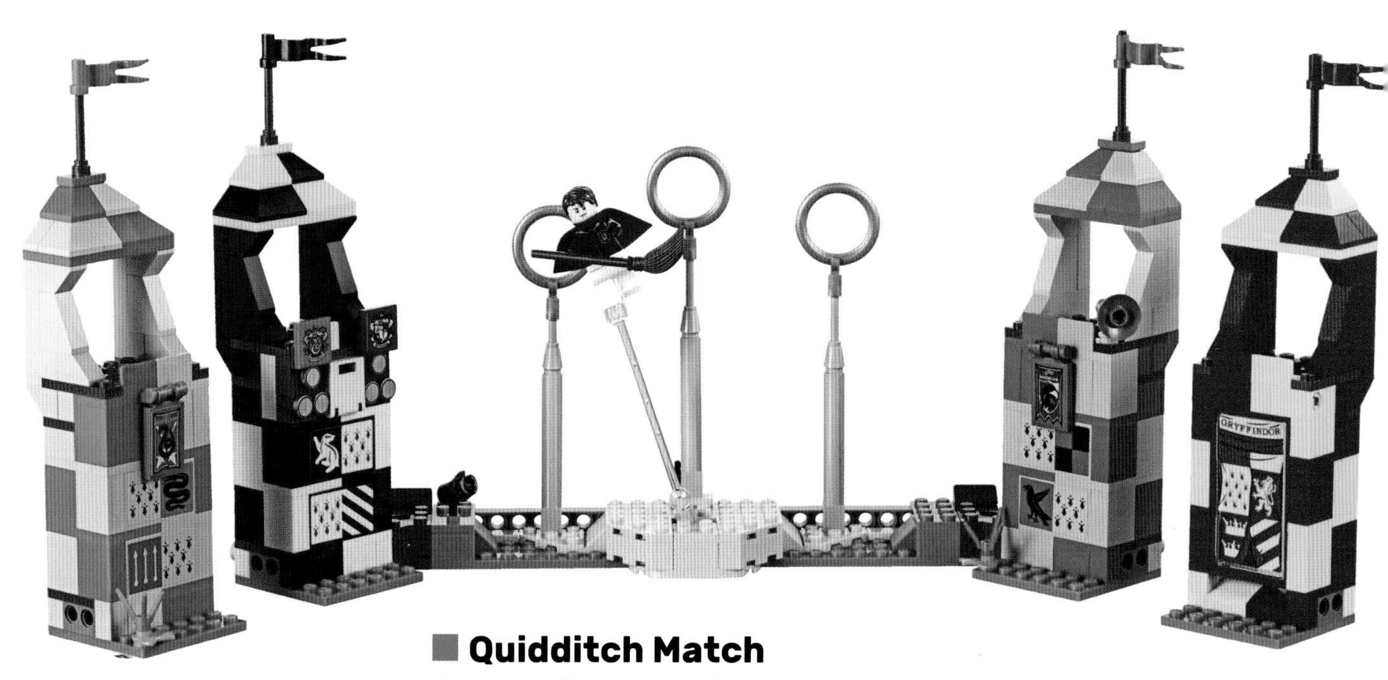

Quidditch Match

Slytherin, Hufflepuff, Ravenclaw and Gryffindor house towers surround the Quidditch pitch at Hogwarts as a broomstick-mounted minifigure protects three goal posts in a classic 500-piece set.

A LEGO brick dragon can be placed atop the castle.

The four Hogwarts founders are included as minifigures for the *Harry Potter* faithful.

Hogwarts Castle

An ambitious undertaking even for LEGO experts, the spires and halls of Hogwarts are even sleeker in LEGO bricks than they are on film. They are, however, no less impressive: The set costs $399.99 and comes with more than 6,000 pieces.

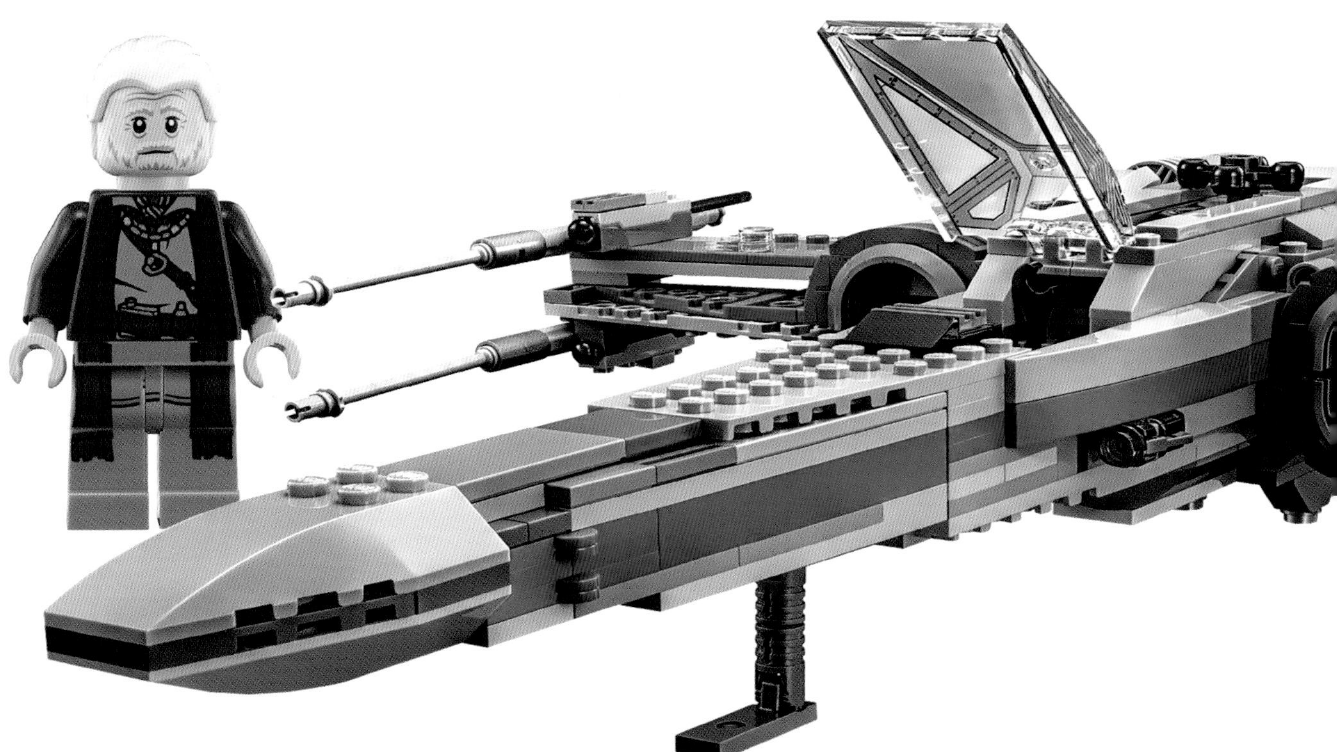

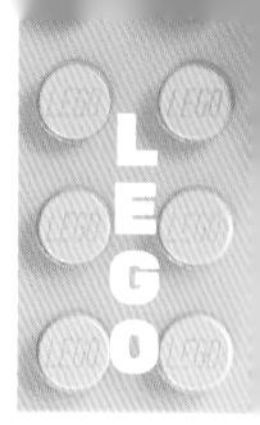

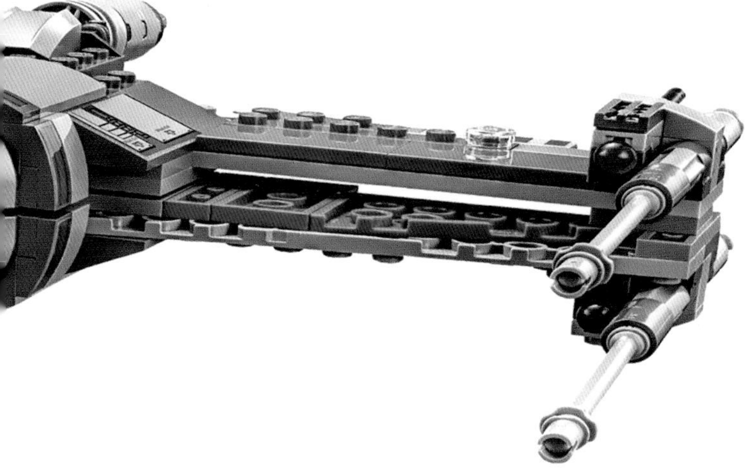

Star Wars: The Force Awakens

The Resistance X-Wing set featured unique blue accents and more than 700 pieces for the Star Wars faithful to recreate. Rey's speeder, above, was also a fan favorite, recalling Luke's speeder from *A New Hope*.

Star Wars: A New Hope

The Ultimate Collector's Series Millennium Falcon is the biggest LEGO set ever created. So even though other LEGO brick versions of the ship can be found, even other UCS sets, fans flocked to get their hands on the more-than-7,500-piece marvel that they've since hailed as one of the finest sets of all time.

LEGO
STAR WARS
ULTIMATE COLLECTOR SERIES
7541 PCS/PZS

Star Wars

The Death Star set featured here (75159) was released in 2016 and is a recreation of the 2008 set inset below. It includes rooms from both the original Death Star and the Death Star II featured in *Return of the Jedi*. It also came with 23 minifigures.

The 2005 Death Star II (10143) was the first LEGO Death Star.

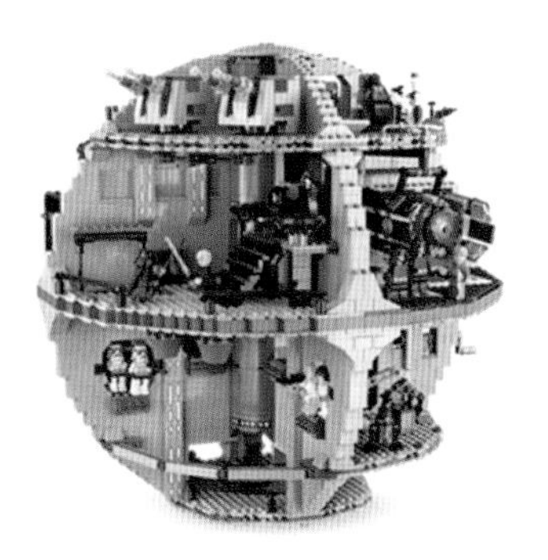

The 2008 Death Star set (10188) was marketed to ages 12 and up until 2010, when that was raised to 14 and up.

LEGO

Celebrating Two Decades

For the occasion of the 20th anniversary of the partnership between the LEGO Group and Lucasfilm, LEGO *Star Wars* has created reimaginings of some of the films' most memorable pieces. Pictured are the Slave I, Snowspeeder, Clone Scout Walker and Anakin's Podracer.

1,007
Number of pieces in Slave I - 20th Anniversary Edition

The Slave I comes with minifigures of bounty hunters Boba Fett, Zuckuss and 4-LOM, as well as Han Solo (and his carbonite slab).

Reimagining Minifigures

Along with each of the five reissued sets, LEGO *Star Wars* included tribute minifigures of Leia, Lando, Darth Vader, Han and Luke on special 20th anniversary stands, offering fans a bonus to add to their *Star Wars* collections.

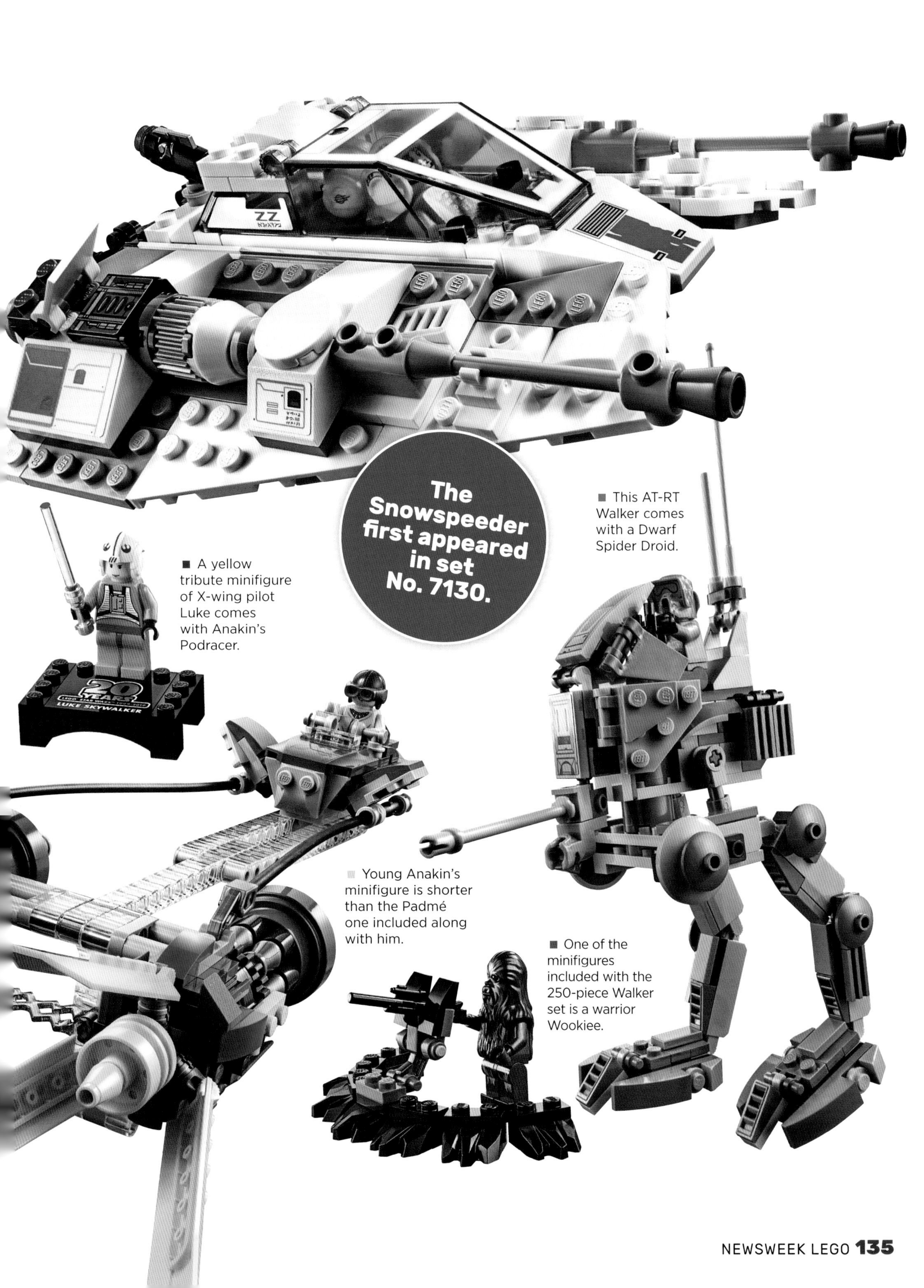

The Snowspeeder first appeared in set No. 7130.

■ This AT-RT Walker comes with a Dwarf Spider Droid.

■ A yellow tribute minifigure of X-wing pilot Luke comes with Anakin's Podracer.

■ Young Anakin's minifigure is shorter than the Padmé one included along with him.

■ One of the minifigures included with the 250-piece Walker set is a warrior Wookiee.

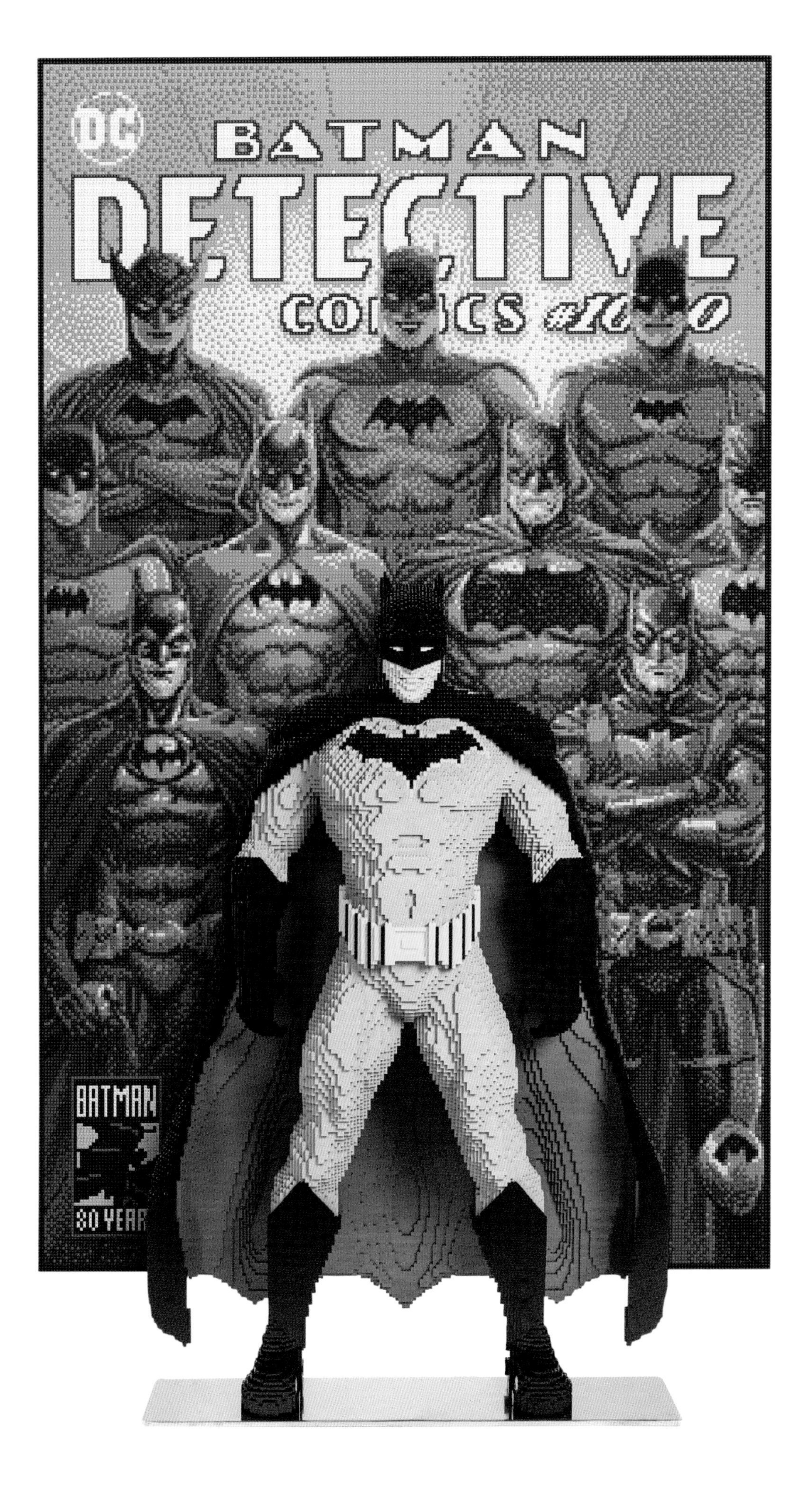

DC
BATMAN
DETECTIVE
BATMAN

In-depth LEGO brick creations Batman, Iron Man and a Sith Trooper were created for San Diego Comic Con. The LEGO booth is always one of the event's highlights.

The Marvel Universse

The Marvel Cinematic Universe is one of the highest-grossing tities in cinema history, so it's no surprise some of the most popular LEGO sets are tied to The Avengers and their many offshoots. Pictured are the Super Hero Airport Battle Iron Man minifigure, S.H.I.E.L.D. Helicarrier and Captain America Civil War Captain Americas Motorcycle Mini Set.

LEGO

LEGO
MARVEL
SUPER HEROES
16+
76042
The SHIELD Helicarrier
64
AVENGERS

DC Comics

With its 2006 and 2017 Classic Batcave set and Wonder Woman Warrior Battle minifigure, the LEGO Group integrated the other comic book behemoth into its cast of branded tie-ins, with an additional boost given to the partnership by *The LEGO Batman Movie*.

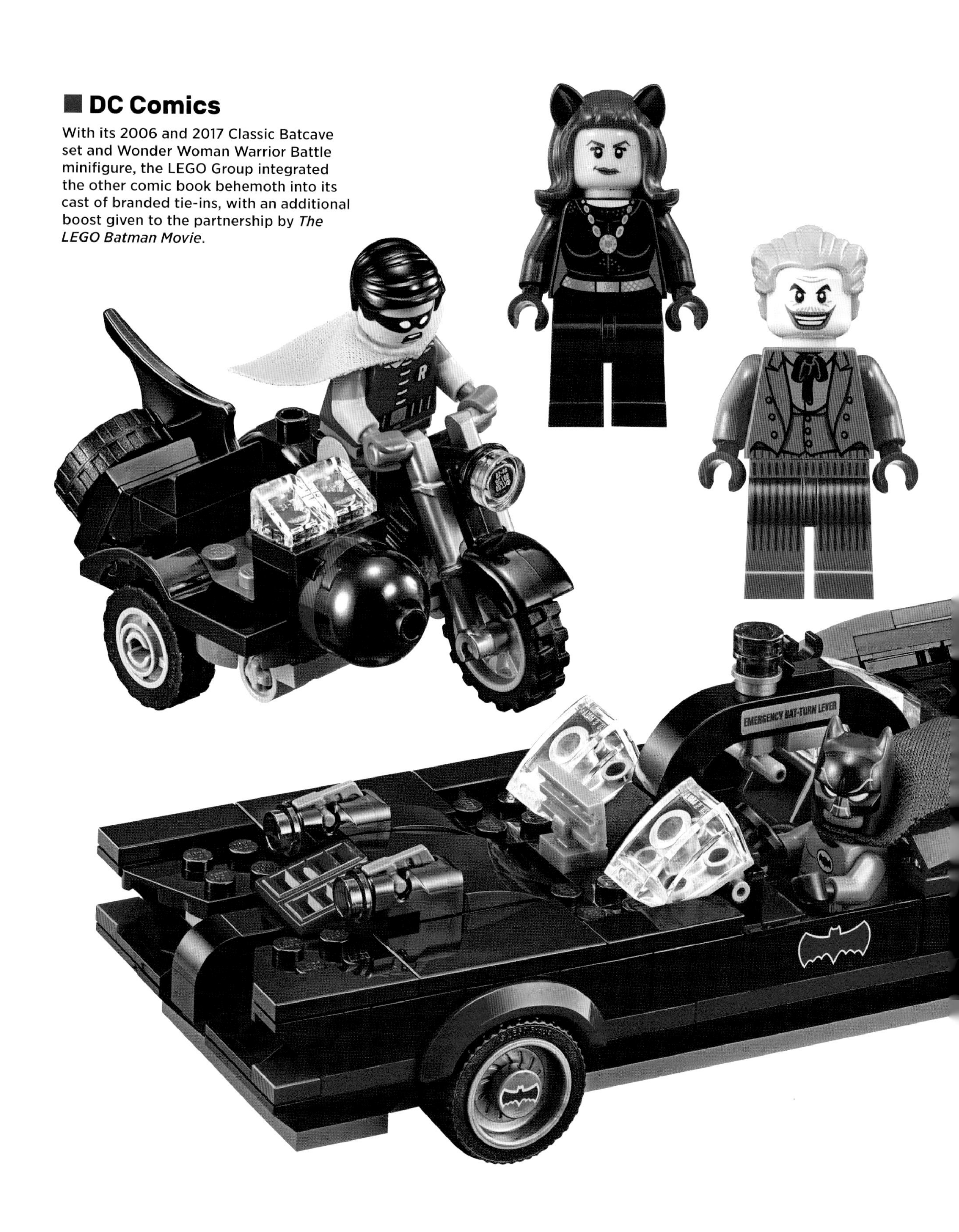

LEGO

LEGO
DC COMICS
SUPER HEROES
6-12
76075
Wonder Woman™
Warrior Battle
DC

LEGO
DC COMICS
SUPER HEROES
14+
76052
Batman™
Classic TV Series
– Batcave
BATMAN

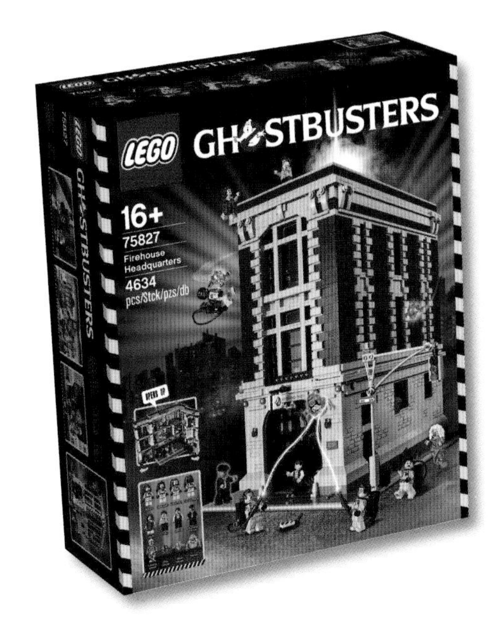

Ghostbusters

When there's something strange in the neighborhood, there's only one team to call—the Ghostbusters. And the LEGO Universe always had the potential for something strange, whether it's a boy wizard, a dinosaur attack or a Slimer assault. So when 2014 saw LEGO brick versions of the Ecto-1 and, in 2016, the famous *Ghostbusters* firehouse, it was a perfect fit.

Stranger Things

The most popular horror series of the streaming age, *Stranger Things* got the LEGO brick treatment in 2019, complete with an "Upside Down" feature that allows the set to be displayed in either direction.

■ Minifigures included the terrifying Demigorgon and tragic fan favorite Barb.

LEGO
THE LORD OF THE RINGS
14+
10237
The Tower of Orthanc

The Lord of the Rings

In 2013, the spikes and shards of Saruman's tower, Orthanc, from the *Lord of the Rings* films, were rendered into LEGO bricks. Complete with a minifigure version of Gandalf escaping on a giant eagle, the set is an impressive ode to a fiction classic. Also pictured as part of the fall of Isengard is Treebeard.

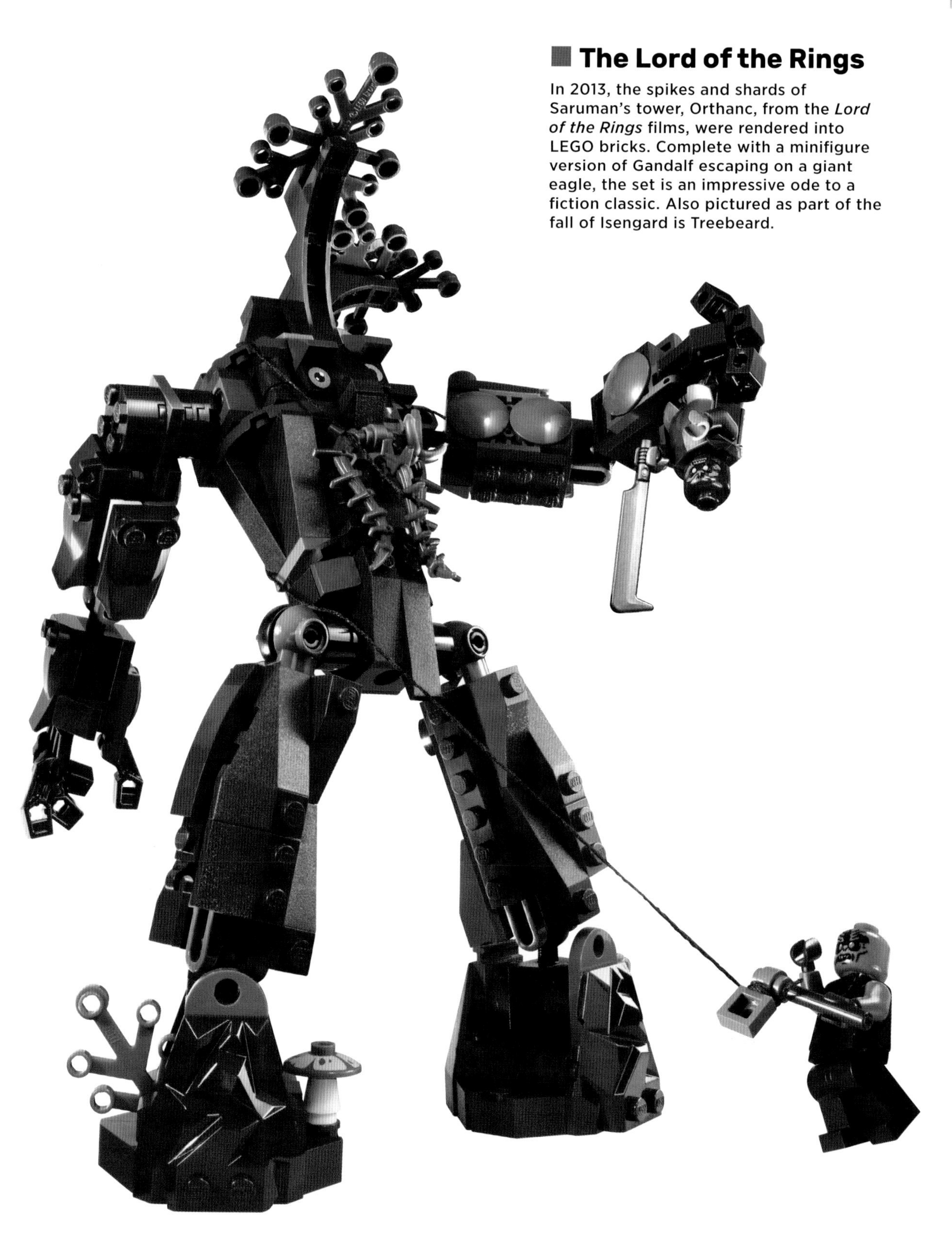

LEGO
JURASSIC WORLD
6-12
75917
VET UNIT
MVU-83
ACU

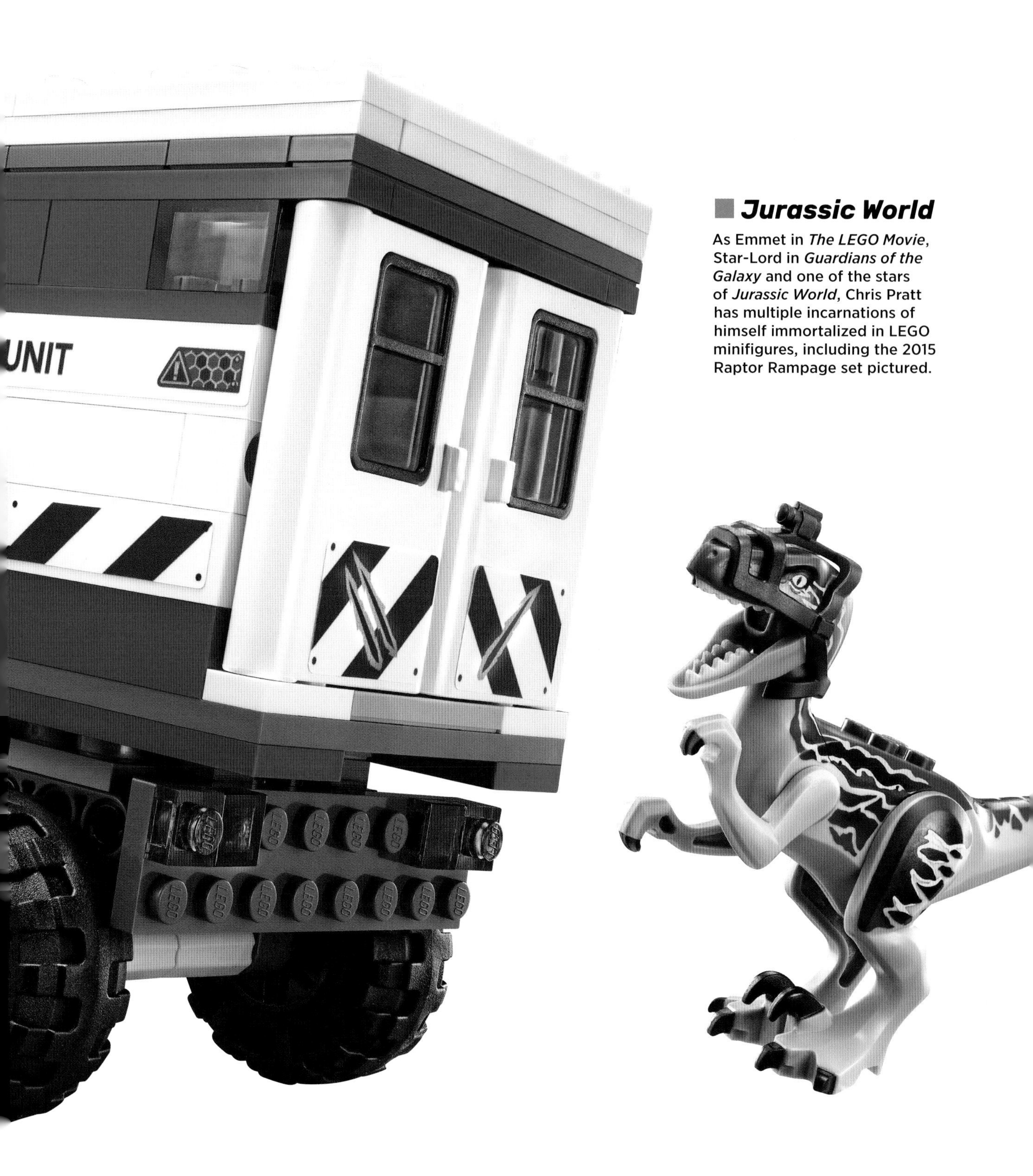

Jurassic World

As Emmet in *The LEGO Movie*, Star-Lord in *Guardians of the Galaxy* and one of the stars of *Jurassic World*, Chris Pratt has multiple incarnations of himself immortalized in LEGO minifigures, including the 2015 Raptor Rampage set pictured.

The Simpsons

The debate over which state *The Simpsons*'s Springfield might be found in has been raging for nearly 30 years, but the family took so well to LEGO bricks in 2014 that Springfield may as well be in Denmark. In addition to the family home (pictured), the show's famous Kwik-E-Mart also received a treatment in LEGO bricks.

LEGO
THE SIMPSONS
12+
71006
The Simpsons™
House
PROPERTY
OF NED
FLANDERS
1PHL07

LEGO

POLICE

Doctor Who

With all of time and space to explore, The Doctor has no doubt seen some incredible things made from LEGO bricks. But in 2015, his TARDIS finally got the LEGO brick treatment, making The Doctor himself a LEGO creation.

TRON: Legacy

Some visual styles are so striking they seem to cry out for the LEGO brick treatment. So while *TRON: Legacy* might not have turned out to be the blockbuster it could have been, LEGO Ideas' version of the iconic Light Cycle bikes should still become a beloved set.

Back to the Future

Complete with Flux Capacitor, the world famous DeLorean from *Back to the Future* got the LEGO Ideas treatment thanks in part to its intense fan base. The 401-piece set includes Marty and Doc Brown minifigures.

Minecraft

The world of *Minecraft* is, with its squared edges and line-based color schemes, particularly well-suited for the LEGO System in Play, and the LEGO Minecraft range has more than 20 sets to offer the dual enthusiast of both the video game and the LEGO system.

Adventure Time

The Land of Ooo was, for fans of the animated show *Adventure Time*, the perfect fit for a LEGO brick remix. The adventures of Jake the Dog and Finn the Human across a whimsical landscape of unbelievable creatures mirrors the LEGO System of Play. Both encourage thinking about everyday things, like shapes and colors, as components in a larger, more imaginative whole.

Indiana Jones

In 2008, the LEGO Group released its *Indiana Jones: The Original Adventures* video game, as well as an Indy minifigure (with hat and whip, of course) and Jeep.

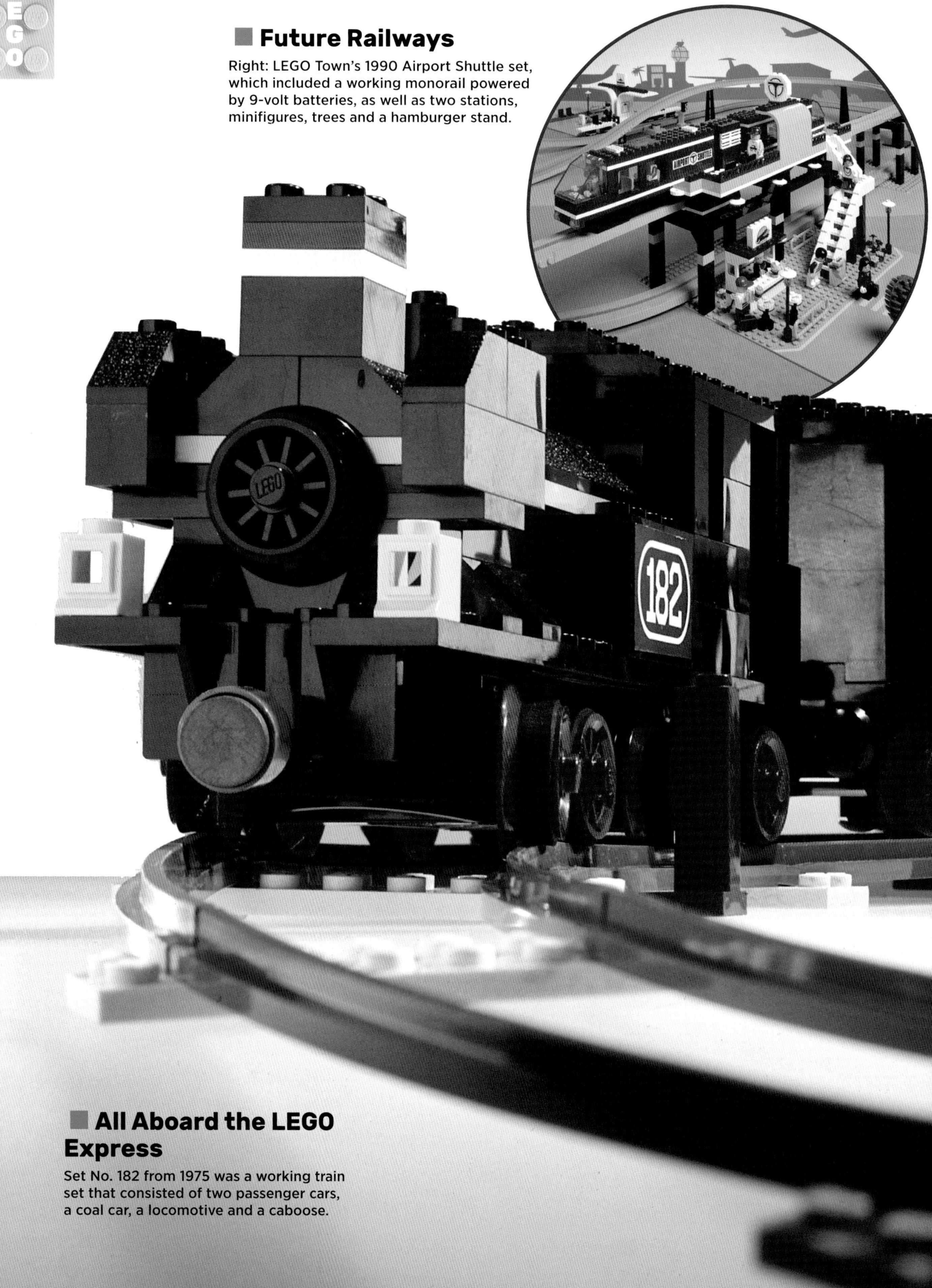

Future Railways

Right: LEGO Town's 1990 Airport Shuttle set, which included a working monorail powered by 9-volt batteries, as well as two stations, minifigures, trees and a hamburger stand.

All Aboard the LEGO Express

Set No. 182 from 1975 was a working train set that consisted of two passenger cars, a coal car, a locomotive and a caboose.

Roads & Rails of the LEGO Universe

LEGO Technic offers builders the chance to recreate real-life elements with remarkable accuracy.

Volvo Concept Hauler PEGAX

A futuristic concept model created in conjunction with Volvo, this construction vehicle can be built one of two ways. This build is a concept hauler in classic Volvo colors.

An aerial view of the hauler build, which measures 15 inches long.

The Volvo Concept Loader will remind some LEGO fans of 2007's classic construction set, the Motorized Bulldozer.

A mapping drone is included with the set, punctuating the probable importance of robotics in future construction projects.

Volvo Concept Wheel Loader ZEUX

In both builds, the Volvo Concept vehicle has four-wheel steering. The set comes with 1,167 pieces, plus Volvo stickers and other decals.

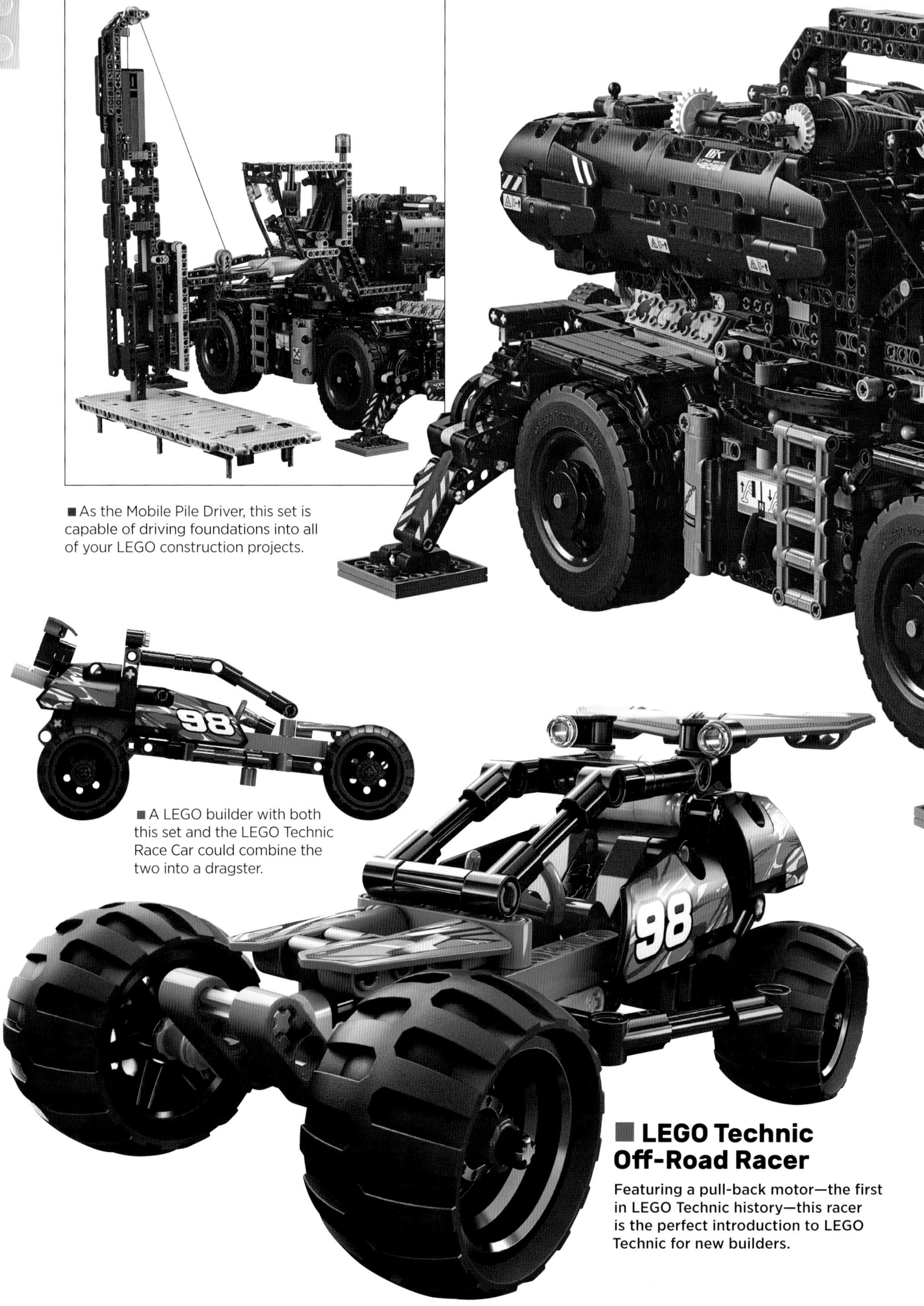

■ As the Mobile Pile Driver, this set is capable of driving foundations into all of your LEGO construction projects.

■ A LEGO builder with both this set and the LEGO Technic Race Car could combine the two into a dragster.

■ LEGO Technic Off-Road Racer

Featuring a pull-back motor—the first in LEGO Technic history—this racer is the perfect introduction to LEGO Technic for new builders.

LEGO Technic Rough Terrain Crane/Mobile Pile Driver

LEGO fans could put their crane operator skills to the test like never before in August 2018 when the Rough Terrain Crane was released, complete with working V8 pistons.

LEGO users can extend the boom on the Rough Terrain Crane more than 3 feet in the air.

LOOKING BACK ON THE LEGO BRICK

Andrea Du Rietz, Senior Manager of Environmental Responsibility at the LEGO Group, on the company's future.

Did you have a background with the LEGO System in Play before you started working there?
My father reassures me that LEGO bricks were a big part of my childhood—just like they were for him. My reintroduction to LEGO bricks happened when I started working here. I did not have kids, or nieces and nephews, at that point that I hung out with. The most difficult thing when starting to play with LEGO again was to let my imagination go wild. I was happy following instructions but uncomfortable with creating something new on my own. It actually was not a specific set that inspired my imagination, but when I participated in our internal Play Agent course. Half a day of learning and playing unlocked something in me and forced me out of my comfort zone, which was a great thing!

What's the best part about being immersed in the LEGO System in Play as a career?
The best bit for me is that it is more than OK (it is encouraged) to have fun at work. Brainstorming is always fun and we are allowed to think like kids. Even though I work in a corporate, strategic role on paper, creativity and imagination is still asked of in my day-to-day work.

If you had to pick just one LEGO set to show to someone with no knowledge of what LEGO bricks could do, which set would it be?
This might be an obvious one coming from me—I sit in the Environmental Responsibility department and work on the LEGO Group's sustainability strategy—but it would be a set with our new elements made from sugarcane. This was our inauguration into the realm of sustainable materials. We released the first bio-based plastic elements in 2018 that were plants (leaves, bushes) made from plants!

Do you have a favorite product line or set? What is it about the set that makes it memorable for you?
I love the super-intricate LEGO Technic builds. I am amazed at what you can create and how they move. I used to love reading appliance manuals as a kid, and this kind of reminds me of that. Our LEGO DC Super Hero Girls sets are another favorite, simply because I love female superheroes. A picture of the Super Hero Girls are both my email and laptop backgrounds!

Is there a minifigure that looks like you?
I am a boxer (and a woman) and boxing is not a female-dominated sport. I therefore love that we made a female boxer minifigure a couple of years ago. She is even a brunette, just like me! Most people in the office know that I box. When the new minifigure came out, before I had even discovered it, our local barista had found one for me and gave it to me for my birthday! He even managed to find one without opening the bag, which is a seriously awesome skillset.

■ LEGO Creator Ferrari

The Ferrari F40 set includes several rare or unique features. The V8 engine and front and rear windshields utilize unusual pieces, and the red race car seats are replicated from the real thing.

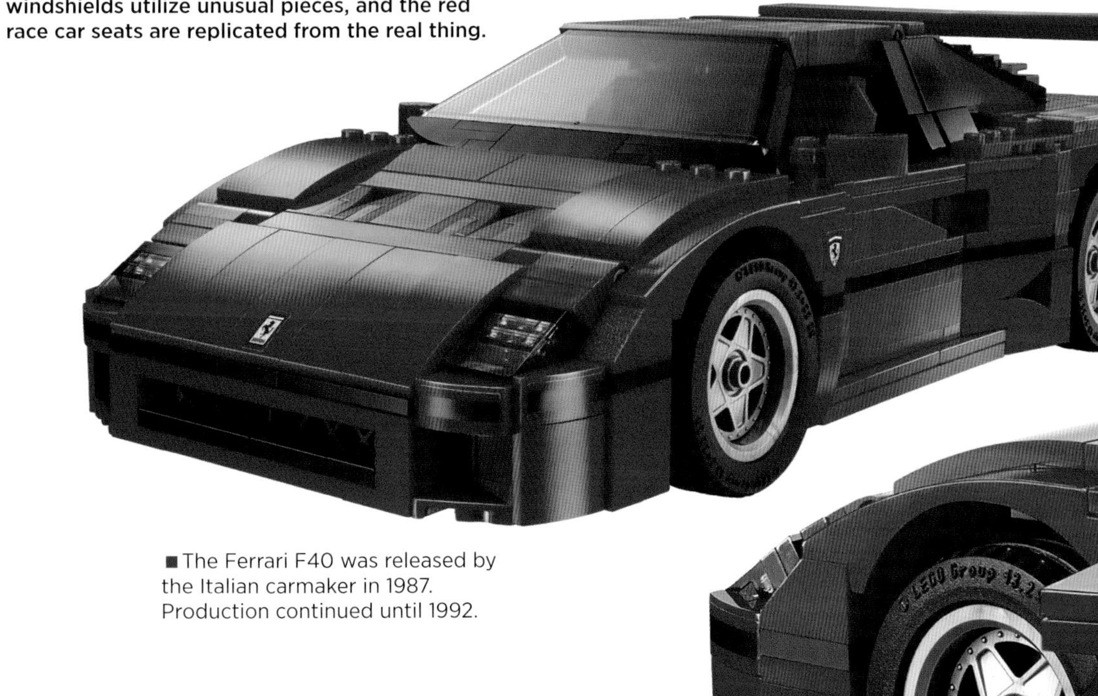

■ The Ferrari F40 was released by the Italian carmaker in 1987. Production continued until 1992.

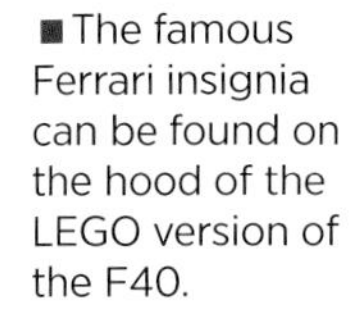

■ The famous Ferrari insignia can be found on the hood of the LEGO version of the F40.

■ Consisting of more than 1,100 pieces, the LEGO Creator Expert Ferrari F40 includes opening doors and hatches.

Ghostbusters Ecto-1

Consisting of 4,634 pieces and with an initial price tag of $349.99, the *Ghostbusters* Firehouse Headquarters set is a massive undertaking for those who can get their hands on one. But the more practical piece is the Ecto-1 set, pictured, which features Ghostbusters minifigures and a LEGO brick version of the most tricked out hearse in history.

Train Time For LEGO Bricks

Clockwise from top left: Locomotive without Motor from 1967; the 1980 LEGO Trains Inter-City Passenger Train set had more than 700 parts and came with 10 minifigures and a departures board; 2013's 1,351-piece LEGO Creator Horizon Express featured rarely used orange bricks and a detachable roof that allowed users to play with the included six minifigures in two passenger cars and a locomotive.

■ Harry Potter and Ron Weasley minifigures push their LEGO brick trolley through King's Cross.

■ Hogwarts Express

Featuring an over-rail bridge to the famous Platform 9¾, the Hogwarts Express set comes with 801 pieces, including a newsstand with copies of *The Daily Prophet*.

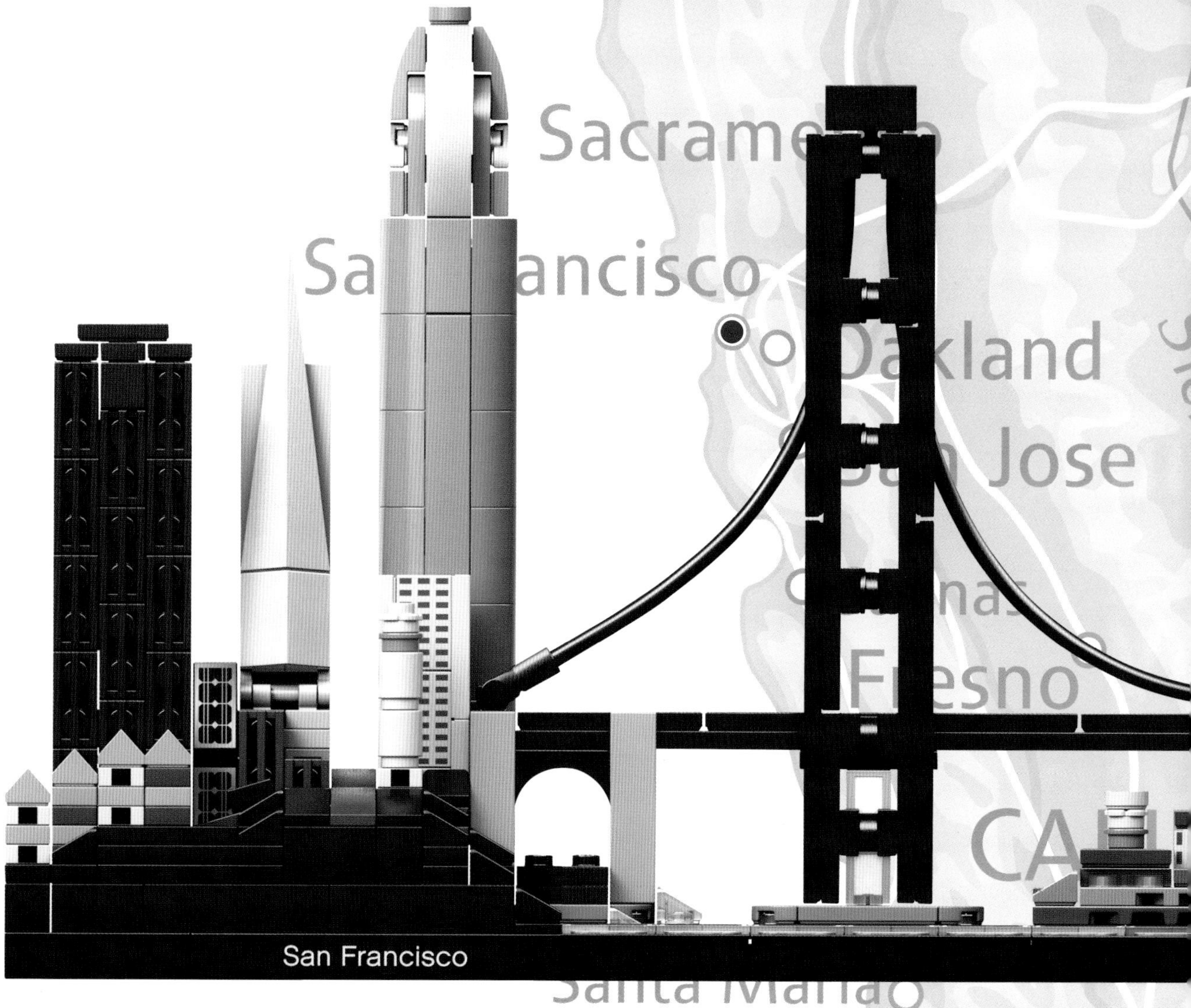

LEGO Across America

LEGO Architecture offers builders the chance to see their favorite architectural marvels in LEGO bricks.

San Francisco

The City by the Bay is one of LEGO Architecture's newest offerings, and the one that inspires Rocco Buttliere, professional artist whose preferred medium is the LEGO brick, who has replicated some of the city's landmarks before as part of his own work. "Something I've always admired about the LEGO Architecture skylines is the way they set the stage for a relatively accurate geographical representation of each city," he says. "San Francisco, I think, embodies this presentation most successfully, not only in terms of the city's unique topography, but especially the way in which forced perspective was achieved in the design of the Golden Gate Bridge. Having designed and built my own 1:650-scale model of the bridge, I know firsthand how daunting the full scale of the span truly is."

Las Vegas

Perhaps no other destination showcases the whimsicality that can be achieved with modern building materials than Vegas. LEGO Architecture's Las Vegas set includes the Bellagio and its famous fountains, the Luxor pyramid, the Wynn Las Vegas and the Stratosphere Tower.

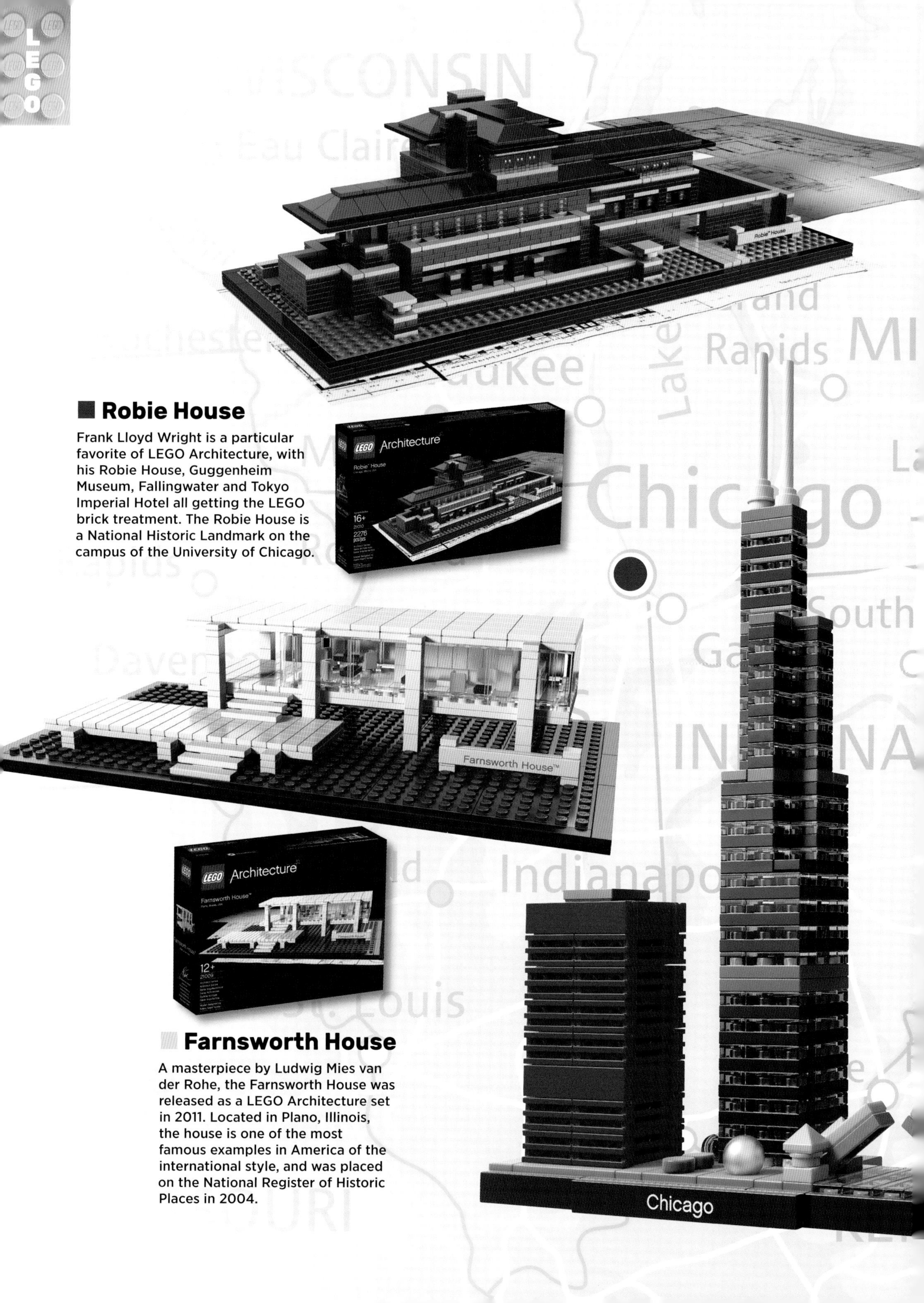

Robie House

Frank Lloyd Wright is a particular favorite of LEGO Architecture, with his Robie House, Guggenheim Museum, Fallingwater and Tokyo Imperial Hotel all getting the LEGO brick treatment. The Robie House is a National Historic Landmark on the campus of the University of Chicago.

Farnsworth House

A masterpiece by Ludwig Mies van der Rohe, the Farnsworth House was released as a LEGO Architecture set in 2011. Located in Plano, Illinois, the house is one of the most famous examples in America of the international style, and was placed on the National Register of Historic Places in 2004.

Fallingwater

Widely considered Frank Lloyd Wright's masterpiece, Fallingwater is a rural estate in Pennsylvania built for Edgar Kaufmann Sr. The LEGO Architecture set, released in 2009, includes 811 pieces.

Chicago

The pearl in America's modernist city crown, Chicago's skyline is a rich look back at America's growth. The LEGO Architecture set includes the Big Red, Cloud Gate (aka "the Bean"), the Willis Tower, DuSable Bridge, the Wrigley Building and the John Hancock Center.

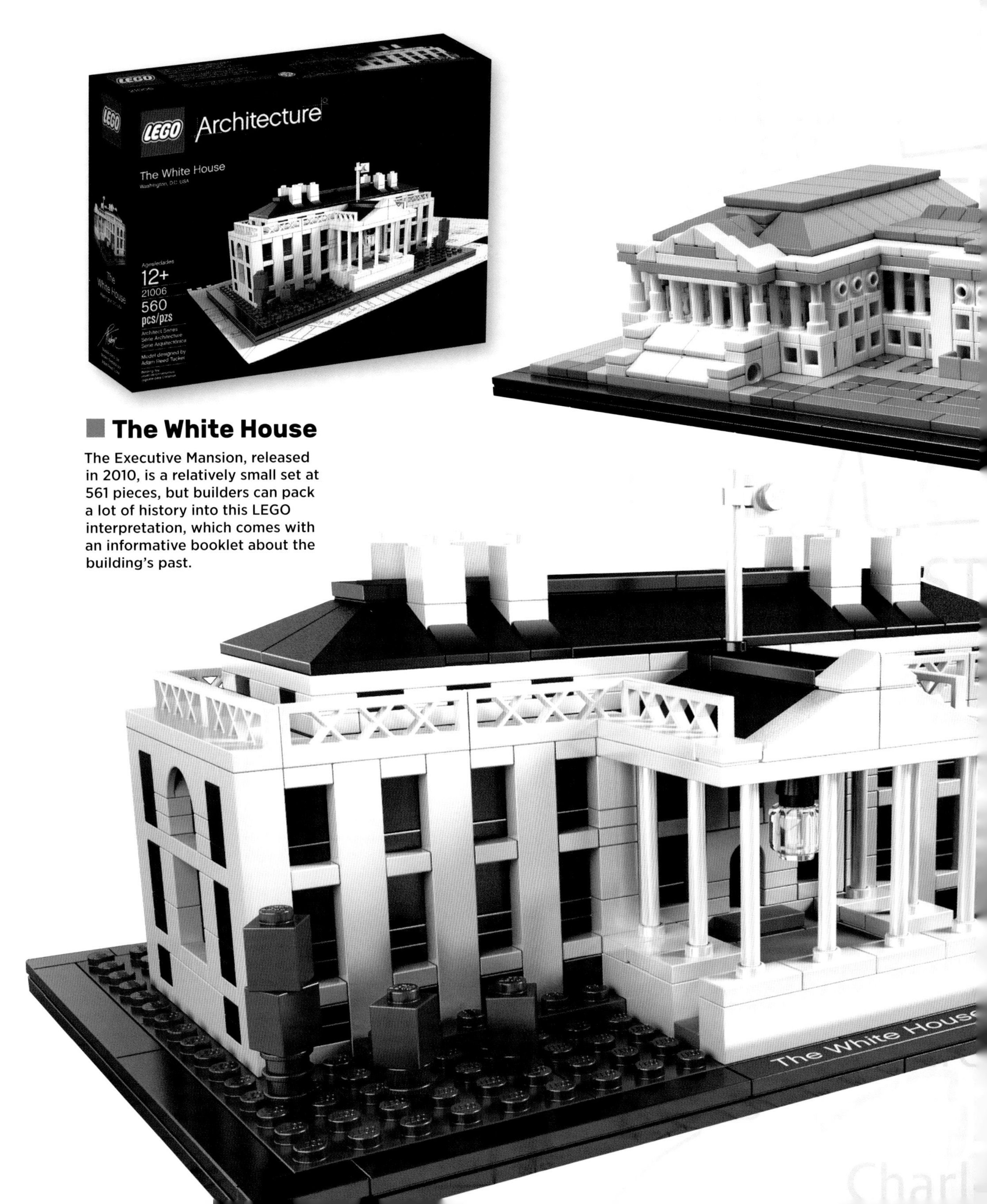

The White House

The Executive Mansion, released in 2010, is a relatively small set at 561 pieces, but builders can pack a lot of history into this LEGO interpretation, which comes with an informative booklet about the building's past.

United States Capitol Building

Featuring a removable dome that offers an aerial view of the inner rotunda, the U.S. Capitol Building is a 1,032-piece set. It focuses on the neoclassical facade of the building, which houses both chambers of the U.S. legislative branch.

Rockefeller Center

A complex of 19 buildings on Fifth Avenue in Manhattan, Rockefeller Center began construction in 1931 and has since become one of the most iconic offices in the world. The LEGO version includes more than 200 mostly tan bricks and creates a distinctly LEGO spin on the buildings.

Solomon R. Guggenheim Museum

With its iconic spiral shape, the Guggenheim Museum in New York is perhaps Frank Lloyd Wright's best-known work, even though he was in his old age when planning began. The LEGO version was released in 2009 for the building's 50th anniversary.

■ New York City

The most famous skyline in the U.S., New York's skyscrapers have welcomed millions of new Americans over the decades, a history reflected in the LEGO set, which includes the One World Trade Center, the Flatiron Building, the Chrysler Building, the Empire State Building and the Statue of Liberty.

Many Faces of the Minifigure

The beloved minifigure celebrates its 40th birthday this year and is more prevalent than ever.

LEGO minifigure heads are produced at the LEGO Group's Hungary factory. Inset: One of the first minifigures was a policeman, updated for the 40th anniversary of the minifigure in 2018 (pictured).

SINCE ITS inception, the LEGO System in Play has been all about building elaborate worlds that people can explore, but in the 1970s the LEGO Group's designers realized their sets were missing a key item: people. The stage had been set, but there were no players. Designer Jens Nygaard Knudsen changed all of that when he brought the first minifigures, including a grinning police officer clad in a sticker uniform, to life in 1978.

These minifigures turned 40 in 2018 and to celebrate, the LEGO Group re-released the Police Officer—with a painted-on uniform this time—along with a whole series dedicated to a party theme. The minifigures could only smile in the '70s, but now they can grimace, smirk and wink, and their costumes go far beyond the boundaries set by their body shape. With his two black eyes and simple smile, the Police Officer looks relatively tame next to Spider Suit Boy and Cactus Girl, a visual testament to how far the LEGO minifigure has come in four decades.

"Over the years we have put much more emphasis on the figures themselves, taking them from generic little plastic civilians to figures which have a wider range of roles, a greater level of detail, a plethora of new accessories and much more personality than they ever had—all to provide a broader array of roleplay experiences," says Matthew James Ashton, vice president of design at the LEGO Group.

Not only are minifigures fun to play with—they're also more coveted than the rarest of action figures. Each new release features an opportunity to present a prime collectible, and the LEGO Group's design team endeavors to give the fans what they want by letting their own imaginations run wild.

"We have a design department of 250 designers who are all brimming with ideas, so there is absolutely no shortage of suggestions on the types of figures we could make in the future," says Ashton. "In fact, we have lists upon lists of different characters we would like to create. We wanted the 40th anniversary LEGO Minifigure series to really feel like a celebration and pull out all the stops to show how cute, silly and fun the figures are."

When creating a new series of original minifigures, a group of designers will sketch some ideas at a brainstorm. According to

"Over the years we have put much more emphasis on the figures themselves, taking them from generic little plastic civilians to figures which have a wider range of roles, a greater level of detail, a plethora of new accessories and much more personality than they ever had."

—MATTHEW JAMES ASHTON, V.P. OF DESIGN AT THE LEGO GROUP

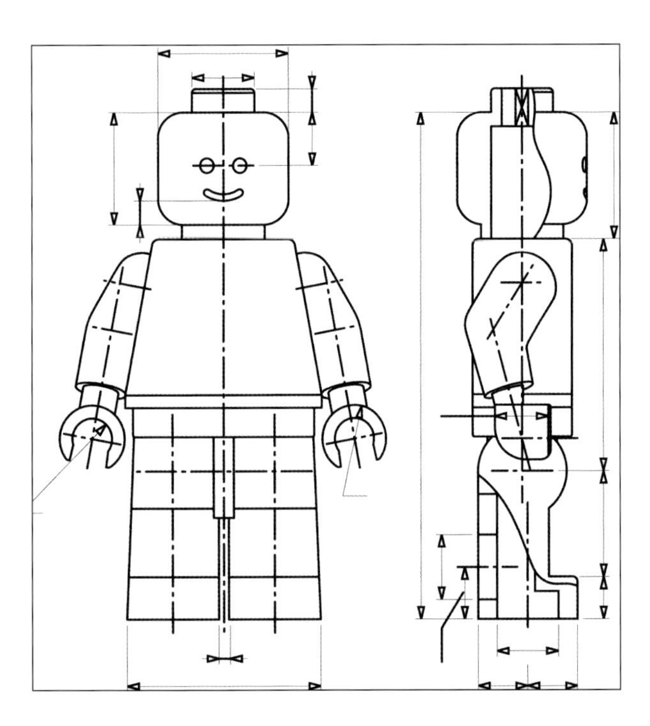

Ashton, the goal in the brainstorming is to always make the most varied line-up of new minifigures possible to appeal to the widest cross section of LEGO fans. The final sketches are then handed off to the graphics and element design team to bring the figments of the design team's imagination into a physical form.

"We are really lucky that the original minifigure was designed in a way that gave us an extremely simplistic figure, which acts as the perfect blank canvas for us to now apply any sort of character," says Ashton. "The figure was originally designed with its functionality probably being pretty high on the design criteria to deliver great roleplay experiences. I would imagine that the original designers had little idea that the figure they created would ultimately turn into such a brand icon."

Iconic is an understatement. Minifigures have become so emblematic that every franchise—from Star Wars to Harry Potter—has rushed to transfer its flesh-and-blood characters into polymer figurines.

Matthew James Ashton works on minifigure designs with a member of his team. Inset: LEGO minifigure construction workers are assembled.

Matthew James Ashton works on the upcoming LEGO Unikitty line with his team. Inset, from left: The factory floor where minifigures are created; Harry Potter minifigures created in 2018.

It's not surprising that fans want little Harry Potters, Hermione Grangers or even Han Solos to play with in their immaculately imagined Hogwarts schools, but the LEGO System in Play also goes to great lengths to incorporate not just the look, but the personality of each character into their respective minifigures.

"When creating licensed characters, we work extremely closely with the movie studios, who will send us specific photos of the characters' costumes, hair styles and accessories," Ashton says. "We will then pass these on to our element design team—who then either hand sculpt and video scan the hair pieces and

accessories, or build them in a computer program, while our graphic design team illustrates the graphics, which will be applied to the minifigure face and body."

The LEGO Group has just released yet another Harry Potter collection (below), featuring new re-creations of scenes and characters. Harry Potter was immortalized in LEGO bricks in 2001 with the Sorting Hat set. The company has grown with the boy wizard and his enduring popularity, and the latest edition of Harry Potter minifigures highlights that relationship. The Hogwarts Castle LEGO set, for example, has hit shelves in various iterations, each more intricate and closer to the film set than the last. Harry Potter and LEGO fans can recreate Harry and Ron's literal run-in with the Whomping Willow, Harry's first Quidditch game and the Hogwarts Express. "With our Harry Potter collectible minifigure line, we will also be introducing brand new poseable short legs, which are perfect for bringing the younger and shorter cast members to life," Ashton says. Avid fans are well on their way to recreating every scene from the eight *Harry Potter* movies entirely through LEGO sets.

Ashton believes adults are so drawn to the minifigures because it reminds them of their first LEGO experience. "I think many adults are extremely nostalgic about their childhood and really like to cling on to those memories, and in some cases relive them," he says. "With the LEGO minifigure being introduced 40 years ago, anyone growing up through the late '70s, '80s or early '90s will have had the opportunity to build and play with LEGO sets and fall in love with the LEGO minifigure as a child. Of course, those little LEGO enthusiasts are all grown up now and quite a few of them are still big kids at heart."

As those big kids continue to have little kids of their own, there's no end in sight for the popular reign of the Minifigure. Here's to another 40 years.

Prototype minifigures like the astronauts, cops and medical professionals at the extreme left of their rows bear little resemblance to the eventual iconic design.

Characters through the years

LEGO minifigures spent the majority of their timeline as simple, yellow-headed and dot-eyed police officers, health care providers and other workers. But they've become an integral part of the LEGO world and have expanded to include some of the most popular franchises in film and TV.

"Minifigures give children an emotional connection to the stories they play out with their LEGO sets. It's so fun to see how these minifigures inspire them to build and play."

—TARA WIKE,
LEGO SENIOR DESIGN MANAGER,
FROM THE BOOK GREAT LEGO SETS

THE WORLD'S BEST BUSINESS CARD

For some lucky workers at the LEGO Group, the minifigure is more than an iconic product—it's a networking tool.

Amy Corbett
Design Manager

Andrea Du Rietz
Senior Manager, Environmental Governance

Tara Wike
Senior Design Manager

Kristian Reimer Hauge
Culture Mediator

Roberta Sandri
Creative Manager

William Thorogood
Vice President of Innovation

Rocco Buttliere's Rome

The LEGO brick artist's 66,000-piece masterwork reimagines the ancient Eternal City.

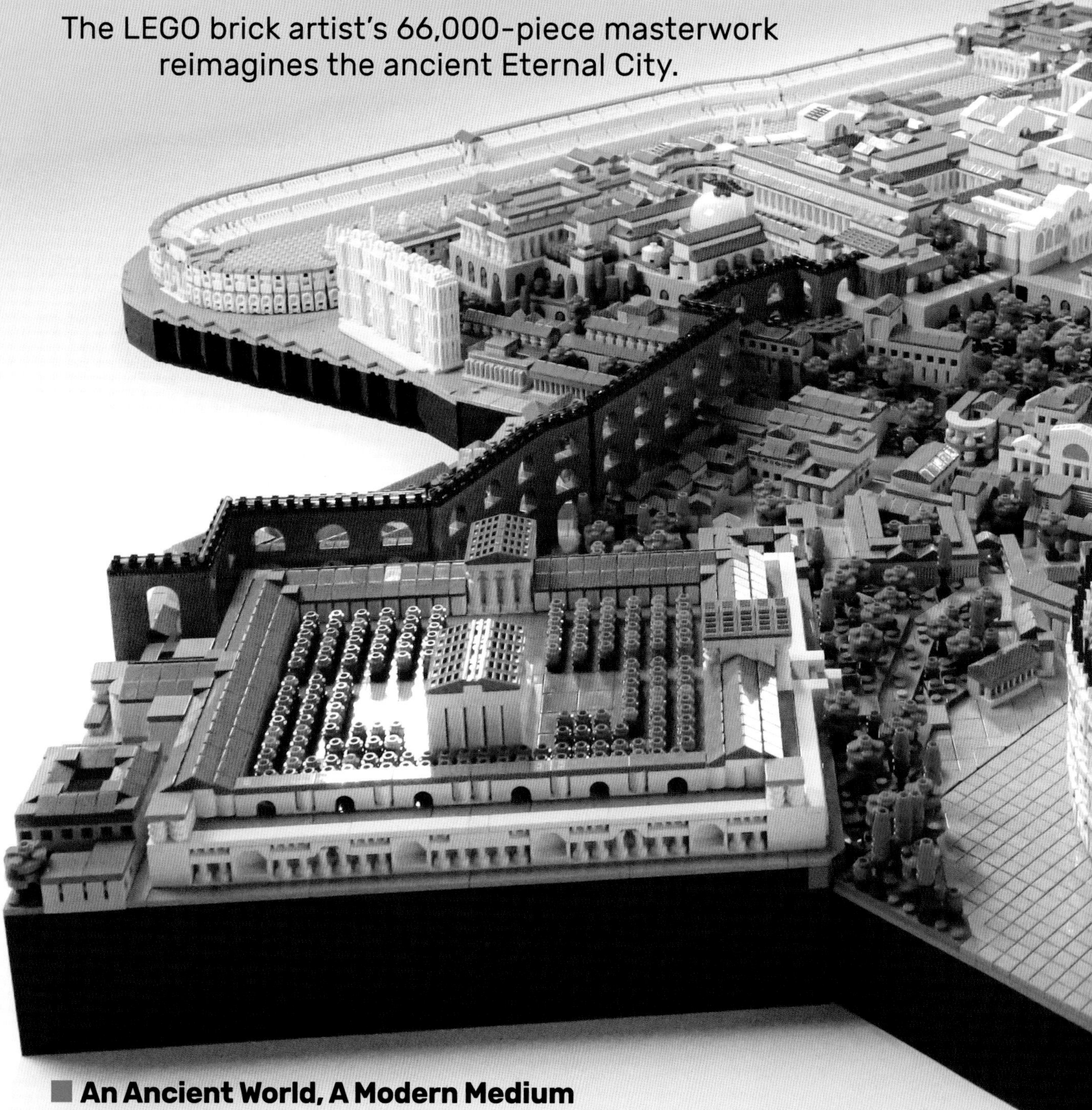

An Ancient World, A Modern Medium

"The basilicas and temples have flashes of lavender and aqua, while the golden friezes of the more prominent temples feature quite unique and seemingly one-use elements as well; such as sink faucets, towball hooks and even frogs!" explains Buttliere. "I certainly enjoyed using a variety of colors which I have never used before throughout the piece. Overall though, what I am most satisfied with is the relative balance of polychromy throughout the piece—specifically, the visual contrast of using tan for the lower-class dwellings and insulae, compared to the gleaming white used to emulate the marble and travertine façades of the public temples, Imperial domūs and theatres."

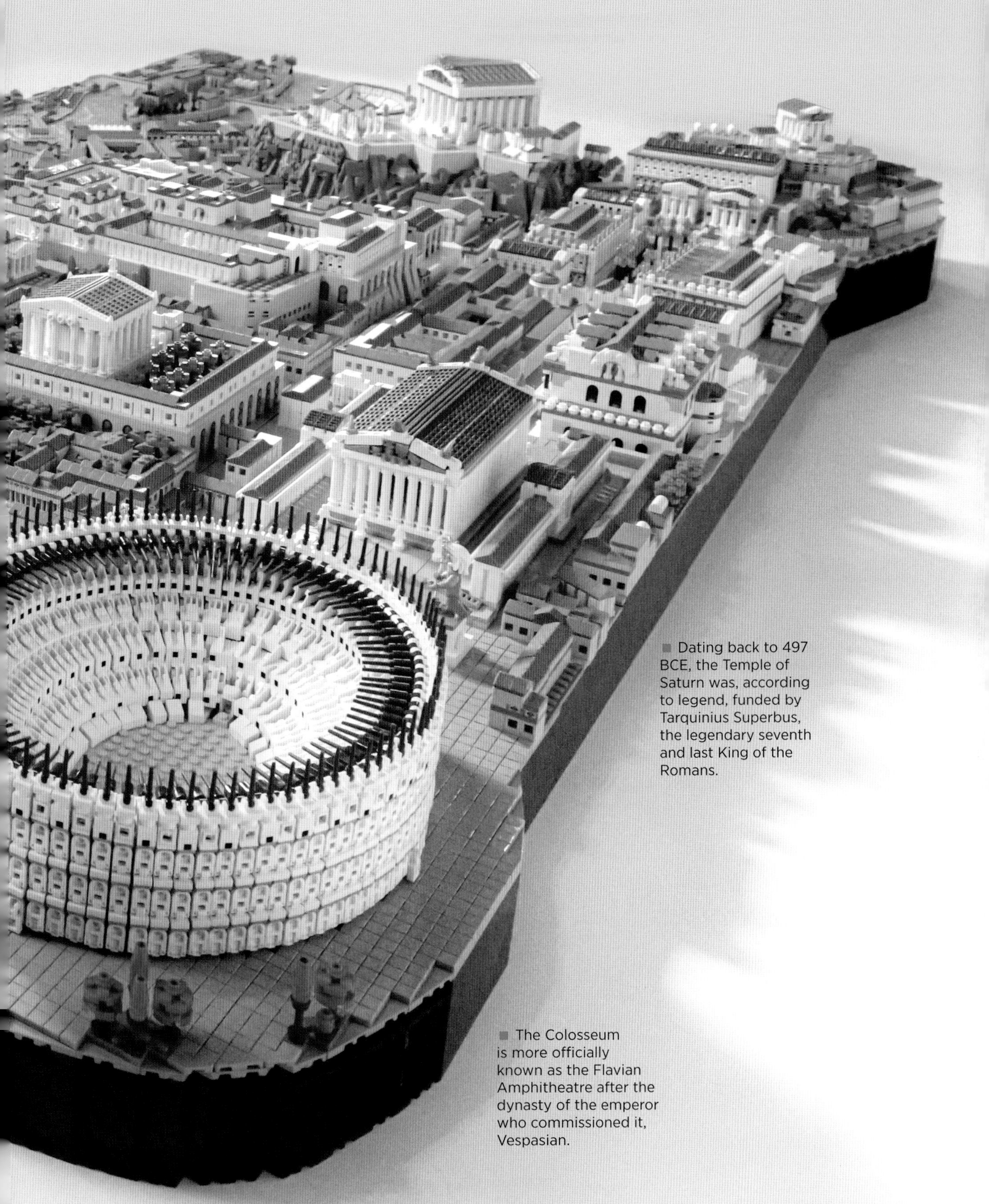

Dating back to 497 BCE, the Temple of Saturn was, according to legend, funded by Tarquinius Superbus, the legendary seventh and last King of the Romans.

The Colosseum is more officially known as the Flavian Amphitheatre after the dynasty of the emperor who commissioned it, Vespasian.

Project of a Lifetime

Crafting timeless pieces of architecture like the Circus Maximus (inset) was a difficult undertaking, even for an accomplished builder like Buttliere. But equally important was showcasing the contrast between the urban congestion of the lower class Rome (right) with the spacious white luxury of hills like the Palatine. "The project was commissioned for the Museu da Imaginação in São Paulo" says Buttliere. "I'll admit to a fair amount of trepidation when I agreed to take on the commission, but it has always been a dream of mine to design a vast city layout in which prominent individual landmarks can be much more realistically portrayed among the surrounding landscape."

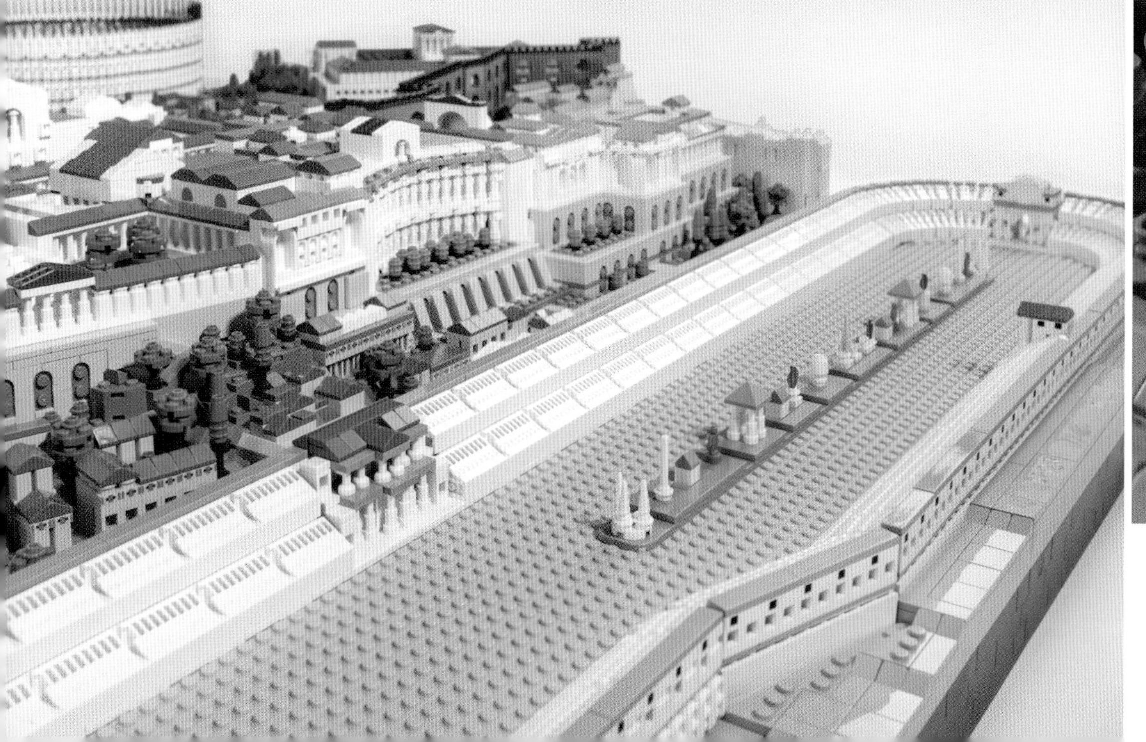

LEGO

President Barack Obama poses alongside a LEGO brick sculpture by artist Nathan Sawaya on the South Lawn of the White House before the start of the South by South Lawn Festival in October 2016.

WHITE HOUSE PHOTO/ALAMY

Topix Media Lab
For inquiries, call 646-838-6637

Published by Topix Media Lab
14 Wall Street, Suite 4B
New York, NY 10005

Printed in China

ISBN-13: 9781948174596
ISBN-10: 1948174596

Cover art: Concept and builds by Nathan Sawaya.
Photos by: Catherine Armanasco/Topix Media Lab: mini figure head.
Christine Bjerke: animals, fruit bowl, gift, the thinker, vase, vehicles, yellow man.
Nathan Sawaya: balls, globe, heart, pizza, treasure chest. Star Wars Death Star and Millenium Falcon courtesy The LEGO Group © 2020.
Digital imaging by Eric Heintz

Photos: Except where noted, All photos courtesy the LEGO Group © 2020
Title Page: Catherine Armanasco/Topix Media Lab; Endpapers: Shutterstock

TM20-03

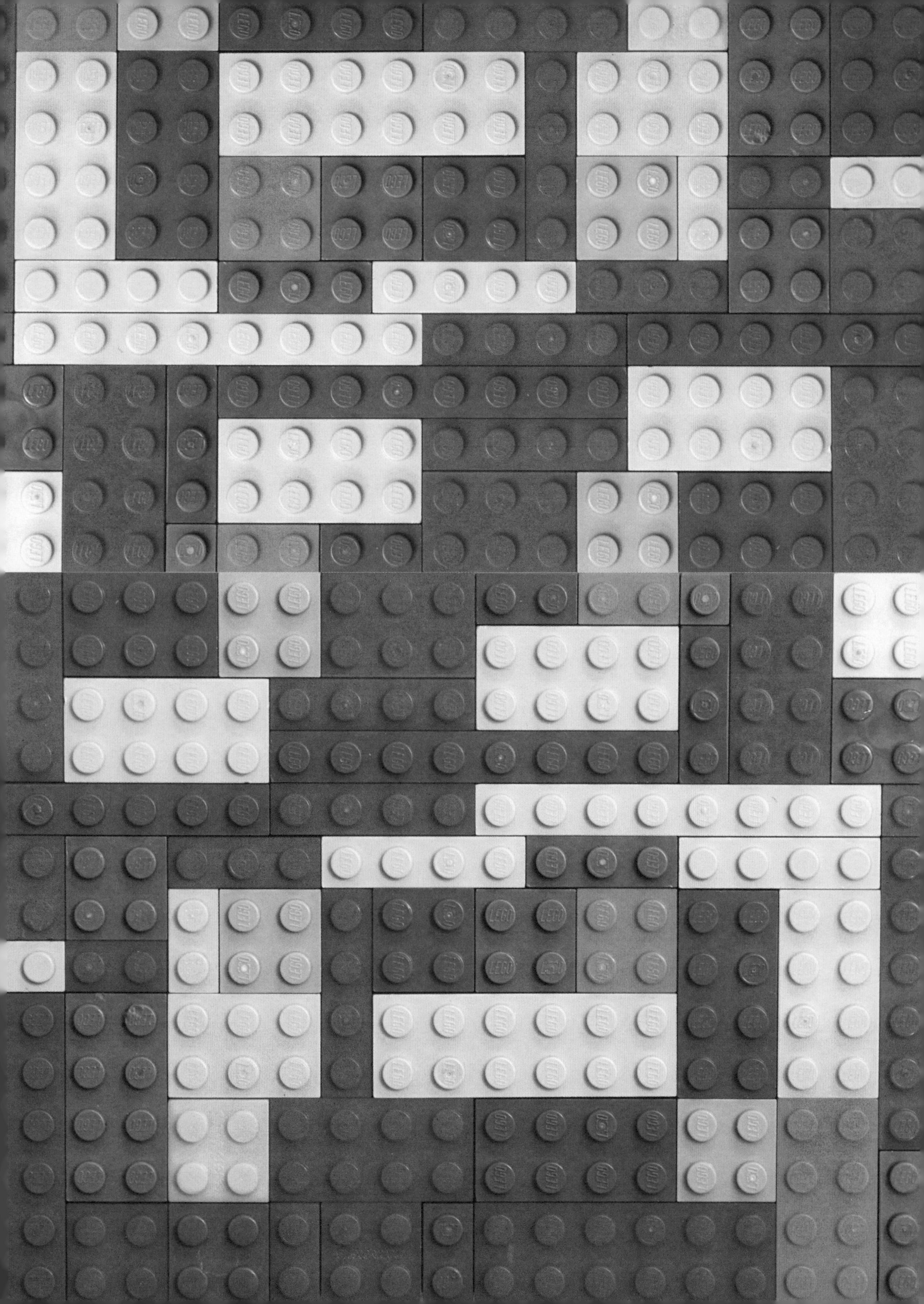

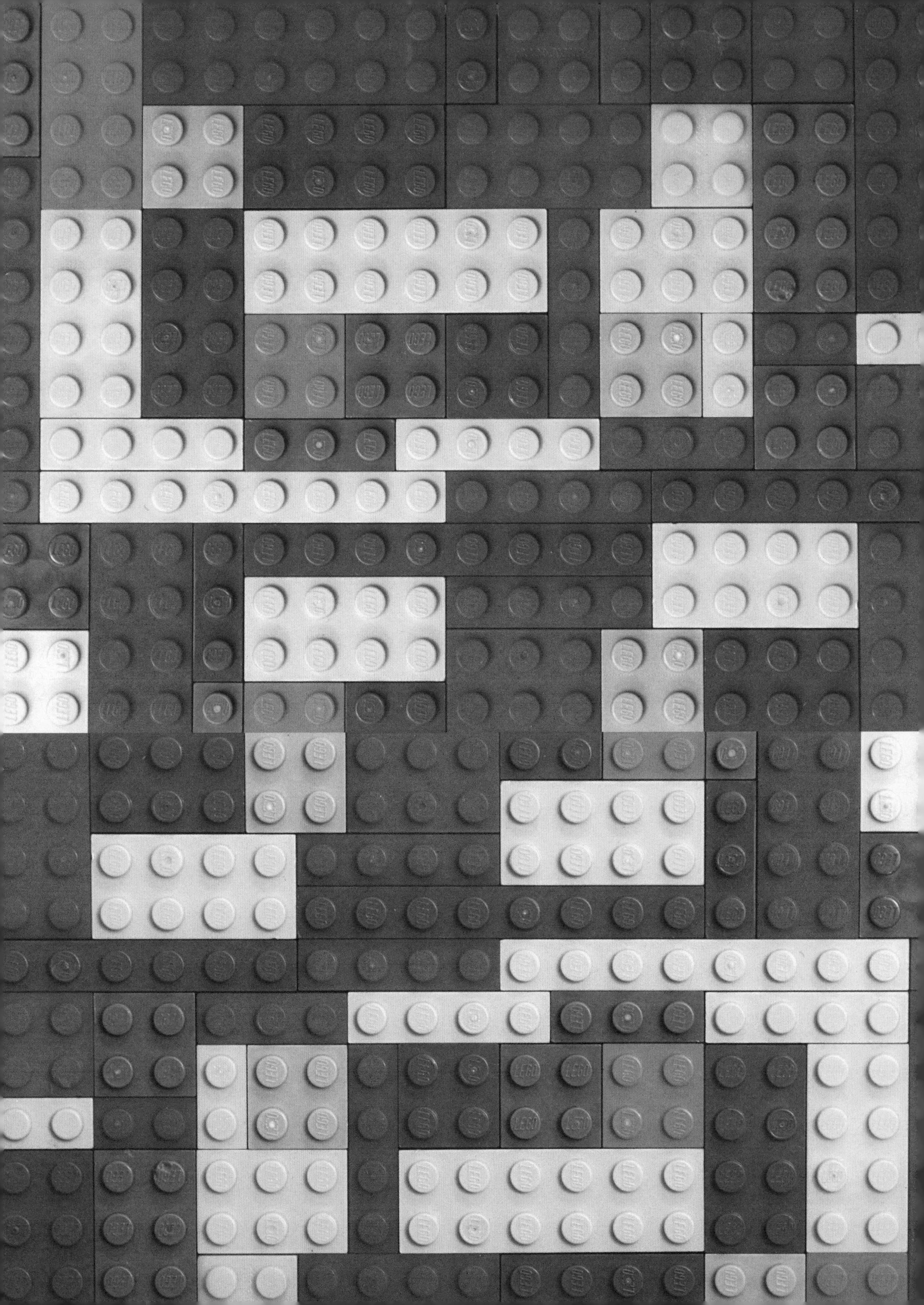